Toni Morrison's

Jazz

Text by
Celeste Bullock
(M.A., New York University)
English Department
The City College of New York, CUNY
New York, New York

Illustrations by
Karen Pica

 Research & Education Association

MAXnotes ® for
JAZZ

Printed in the United States of America

Library of Congress Catalog Card Number 95-72119

International Standard Book Number 0-87891-023-9

MAXnotes ® is a registered trademark of
Research & Education Association, Piscataway, New Jersey 08854

What **MAXnotes®** *Will Do for You*

This book is intended to help you absorb the essential contents and features of Toni Morrison's *Jazz* and to help you gain a thorough understanding of the work. The book has been designed to do this more quickly and effectively than any other study guide.

For best results, this **MAXnotes** book should be used as a companion to the actual work, not instead of it. The interaction between the two will greatly benefit you.

To help you in your studies, this book presents the most up-to-date interpretations of every section of the actual work, followed by questions and fully explained answers that will enable you to analyze the material critically. The questions also will help you to test your understanding of the work and will prepare you for discussions and exams.

Meaningful illustrations are included to further enhance your understanding and enjoyment of the literary work. The illustrations are designed to place you into the mood and spirit of the work's settings.

The **MAXnotes** also include summaries, character lists, explanations of plot, and section-by-section analyses. A biography of the author and discussion of the work's historical context will help you put this literary piece into the proper perspective of what is taking place.

The use of this study guide will save you the hours of preparation time that would ordinarily be required to arrive at a complete grasp of this work of literature. You will be well prepared for classroom discussions, homework, and exams. The guidelines that are included for writing papers and reports on various topics will prepare you for any added work which may be assigned.

The **MAXnotes** will take your grades "to the max."

Dr. Max Fogiel
Program Director

Contents

**Each Part includes List of Characters,
Summary, Analysis, Study Questions and
Answers, and Suggested Essay Topics.**

Introduction

The Life and Work of Toni Morrison

Toni Morrison, a premier contemporary American novelist, chronicles the African-American experience. Morrison has written six novels and a collection of essays and lectures. Her work has won national and international acclaim and has been translated into 14 languages. Her writing has been described as lyrical and she has been applauded for "writing prose with the luster of poetry."

Morrison won the prestigious Pulitzer Prize in 1988 for her novel *Beloved* and the coveted Nobel Prize for Literature in 1993. In a released statement, the Nobel Prize Committee of the Swedish Academy awarded the prize to Morrison "who in novels characterized by visionary force and poetic import, gives life to an essential aspect of American reality."

She is the first African-American writer to win the Nobel Prize, the first American woman to win in 55 years, and the eighth woman to win since the Nobel Prize was initiated in 1901.

Morrison's work, however, is not without controversy. In 1988, 48 African-American writers signed a letter protesting that her novel *Beloved* was overlooked for the National Book Award and the National Book Critics' Circle Award. Many white authors and even some male African-American authors complained when she was selected for the Nobel Prize. They felt she received these awards due to preferential treatment based on race and sex.

However, an overwhelming majority of the literary community agrees that such allegations are without merit. "The Nobel Prize in Literature is not awarded for gender or race," says Nadine Gordimer, the last woman to win the prize in 1991. "If it were, many thousands of mediocre writers might qualify. The significance of Toni Morrison's winning the prize is simply that she is recognized internationally as an outstandingly fine writer."

Often the controversy surrounding such prizes are due in part to fierce competition for the money and prestige that are guaranteed to the recipients. Morrison has been hailed by experts for her ability to "re-imagine the lost history of her people. Others have recognized the Faulknerian influences in her work or that her plots have the sorrow of Greek tragedies. Along with the honor of winning the the Nobel Prize comes a cash award of $825,000. Morrison is currently the Robert F. Goheen Professor in the Council of the Humanities at Princeton University.

Toni Morrison was born Chole Anthony Wofford in Lorrain, Ohio in 1931 during the Great Depression. (Toni is her nickname; Morrison is the name of her ex-husband.) Her grandparents were former sharecroppers who migrated north from Alabama in 1910 to find a better life. Her family's life was not without economic and racial hardships.

They lived in a largely all-white town. Unpleasant memories of growing up there include being looked down upon because she was black. The only part-time job she could get at age 13 was cleaning people's homes. In spite of these humble origins, Morrison received a B.A. from Howard University and a M.A. in English from Cornell University. Her master's thesis was on writer William Faulkner, another Nobel Prize winner, whose work focused on life in the South.

Upon graduation, one of her first round of jobs was teaching at Howard University. One of her students included writer Claude Brown who asked her to look at his 800 page manuscript. His book went on to become the classic urban autobiography *Manchild in the Promised Land.*

Another one of her students who went on to fame was Stokely Carmichael, a student activist and leader in the Black Power Movement of the sixties. In fact, the idea for her first book, *The Bluest Eye,* came from the popular slogan "Black is Beautiful." Morrison placed a twist on that theme by focusing on a little black girl who did not think she was beautiful.

After her teaching stints and the end of her marriage, she raised two sons as a single parent and wrote in her spare time. Morrison was hired by Random House, where she advanced from textbook editor to the position of senior editor. During her 18-year tenure, she helped writers to clean up their manuscripts, edited the *Black Book*, a collection of African-American memorabilia, and pushed for the publication of works by deserving, but often overlooked, African-American authors.

Some of the authors that came to the limelight under her stewardship were Alice Walker, Gayle Jones, Gloria Naylor, and Toni Cade Bambara. Continuing to use Morrison as a guide, African-American female authors have emerged as a consistent and critical dimension in literature.

In a 1994 interview with *Time* magazine, Morrison understands the significance of her work for female authors. "I felt I represented a whole world of women who either were silenced or who had never received the imprimatur of the established literary world. ...Seeing me up there might encourage them to write one of those books I'm desperate to read."

Before Morrison, the most successful African-American writers were males. For example, the work of acclaimed African-American novelist and essayist James Baldwin had tremendous literary impact in the fifties and sixties. Racial themes were explored as they had never been before in his books *Nobody Knows My Name* and *Go Tell It on the Mountain*. Eventually, Baldwin felt uncomfortable living as a second-class citizen in the United States and became an ex-patriate who lived and worked from Paris.

Richard Wright, Baldwin's predecessor, was also an ex-patriate. Beginning with his autobiography *Black Boy* in 1945, Wright continued with *Outsiders*, *Uncle Tom's Children*, and his most important work *Native Son*. Ralph Ellison wrote only one book. Yet Ellison's *Invisible Man* won a National Book Award in 1952 and this allowed him to join the ranks of male authors successful at depicting the disenfranchisement of the African-Americans in the United States.

Morrison is recognized as the most distinguished African-American novelist since Wright, Ellison, and Baldwin. In her work as an author, Morrison wanted to continue to broaden the perspective of American literature by telling the stories she felt were never told, stories about African-American girls and women and the racial and social pressures they faced. She wanted to write about people with the sensibilities of the culture she grew up in. Morrison wanted her work to focus on the joys and sorrows of their lives.

She wrote her first novel when she was in her 30s. *The Bluest Eye*, published in 1970, is about a black girl who feels she has no beauty. If only her eyes were blue and her skin was white, then she could be someone who could be loved. The book received respectable attention. *The Bluest Eye* became the first of many of Morrison's explorations into the identity, self-esteem, and impact of racial discrimination on what she believes to be the most vulnerable—women and children.

Sula, published in 1973, shows two friends, black and female, and how they fit and don't fit into their community. With the publication of *Song of Solomon* in 1977, Morrison won critical and commercial success and the National Book Critics' Circle Award. By the time her next novel *Tar Baby* was due in the bookstores in 1981, she was featured on the cover of *Newsweek*.

Ever expanding on the theme of telling stories untold, it is said her book *Beloved* was written in memory of the millions of lives lost during slavery. The plot centers around an ex-slave Sethe who would rather kill her own children than risk that they be re-enslaved. The ghost of Sethe's dead child tries to remain close to her mother and wreaks havoc when she cannot. All of the characters in *Beloved*, Morrison's Pulitzer Prize winning novel, try to recover from the personal and collective indignities of slavery.

"I was trying to make it a personal experience," says Morrison in a question and answer interview with *Time* magazine. "The book was not about the institution—Slavery with a capital S. It was about these anonymous people called slaves. What they do to keep on, how they make a life, what they're willing to risk, however long it lasts, in order to relate to one another—that was incredible to me," she says.

In 1992 Morrison published *Playing in the Dark*, a collection of her Harvard lectures. In this collection she coins a new term, once again reinventing an already established concept. She teaches a humanities course that changes the term African-American to

American Africanisms. This same year she also published *Race-ing Justice, En-Gendering Power,* essays on the controversy surrounding the Clarence Thomas Supreme Court confirmation hearings.

In her novel *Jazz,* also published in 1992, Morrison continues her theme of giving a voice to the voiceless. Once again, she does everything she can to stretch the imagination. The novel makes both racial and historical statements about the inequities of life for African-Americans in the post-slavery era.

With the writing of *Jazz,* Morrison takes on new tasks and new risks. *Jazz,* for example, doesn't fit the classic novel format in terms of design, sentence structure, or narration. Just like the music this novel is named after, the work is improvisational. In this work, she is influenced not only by the jazz, blues, and gospel music she was reared on, but also by the folklore, tall tales, and ghost stories that her family told for entertainment. The result is a writing style that has a unique mix of the musical, the magical, and the historical.

Historical Background

Jazz takes place in Harlem, New York during the late 1920s. The twenties is a period known in the United States as "The Age of Prosperity." At the end of World War I in 1918, "The war to end all wars," America breathed a sigh of relief, as a collective effort freed the world from German imperialism.

After helping to make the world safe for democracy, there were celebrations nationwide. Americans were eager to refocus their attention on themselves. As a result, the country experienced a growth spurt. Modernization brought the invention of the automobile, an increase in the standard of living, in economic opportunities, and in leisure time.

There was a new way of living. For the first time people worked less hours per week and there was more money to spend on entertainment and conveniences. Appliances like irons, washing machines, and vacuum cleaners were widely available. Canned foods and commercial bakeries freed women from long hours in the kitchen. Movies, baseball games, and sports of every sort were popular.

A new emphasis was placed on education. More children attended school regularly with the goal of completing their educations. An education reform movement called for going beyond the three R's to a more progressive approach.

The political and social climates were pushed in all different directions. The twenties brought the end of the ideals of the Wilson Era.

The presidency passed from Warren G. Harding to Calvin Coolidge to Herbert Hoover. The Eighteenth Amendment to the Constitution prohibited the sale of liquor. Yet, while prohibition was in effect, speakeasies and night clubs, where liquor was sold, were fashionable and in abundance. It is believed that there were over 30,000 speakeasies in New York City and over 200,000 speakeasies in the United States.

The Women's Suffrage Movement pushed for the right to vote, and the Nineteenth Amendment to the Constitution was ratified in 1920. Women formed the League of Women Voters and continued their fight for equality and a change in the status quo.

Change took place very rapidly in all aspects of life. Women's fashions went from just inches off the ground to above the knee. There was new music, new money, and a new carefree attitude. Writers like F. Scott Fitzgerald and Ernest Hemingway best described the mindset of this era. Gaiety and youth were the new ideals and everyone did a wild and crazy dance called the Charleston.

Another important phenomenon of the twenties was the New York Stock Exchange. People had extra money to invest and putting money in stocks was considered a good way to save for the future. Eventually greed, speculation, and a manipulation of the trading system began to have a devastating effect on the economy. Inflation increased and stock prices fell. On October 29, 1929 the stock market crashed. Many experts view this day as the official end of the "Age of Prosperity."

In the twenties African-Americans never fully benefited from the "Age of Prosperity." African-Americans who fought in World War I looked forward to their own taste of freedom. When black soldiers returned home, they wanted freedom from the cotton fields they were still tied to. Under the sharecropping system, no matter how hard they worked, they found themselves deeper and deeper in debt.

After slavery was abolished, African-Americans were no longer forced to pick crops like cotton and sugar cane. However, the work still had to be done, and people still needed a place to live. A land or plantation owner built shacks on his land and the people who picked the cotton or cane crop were allowed to live there. They were given staples like flour, sugar, and perhaps a mule and some tools.

Instead of being paid for the work that was done, another system was devised. The owner would keep a record of how many pounds of cotton were picked, how much rent was charged for the shack, and how much money was owed for the supplies that were given at the start of the year.

Families could work from sun up to sun down for a full year and at the end of the year find themselves getting no pay at all. Furthermore, they found themselves owing the landowner hundreds and hundreds of dollars. Usually sharecroppers could not read or write and were cheated. Prices for the staples were inflated, and prices paid for the crops that were picked were extremely low.

Sharecroppers found themselves doing backbreaking work year after year with nothing to show for it but a growing debt. Children didn't go to school because they had to help bring in the crop. Sharecroppers were often hungry because they didn't make enough money to feed their families and had little time to plant a garden.

Sharecroppers were often sick because the shacks offered very little protection from the heat and the cold. The situation became another form of slavery. When work opportunities opened in the North, southern African-Americans ran away from their debt to start over. The work available in the North, although not glamorous, was much easier than the work they were accustomed to, and they would get paid.

Another concern for African-Americans during the post-slavery era was lynchings. Even though it was 50 years after the end of slavery, lynchings were common in the South. Southern whites were angry about the end of slavery and the gains being made by African-Americans. The Ku Klux Klan, for example, was formed with the purpose of forcefully putting African-Americans back in their place.

The main tactic used by the Klan was terrorism. Klan members would hold night meetings with the faces of those present covered with white hoods to hide their identities. Often Klan members were also important members of the community like the sheriff, the judge, the mayor, and local businessmen.

After exciting themselves at the meeting with anti-African-American talk, they would ride off to an African-American family's home and burn a 10 foot tall cross in the yard. Then the Klan would charge into the house and drag out the father or another male in the family, beat him, castrate him, and hang him from a tree until dead. Women and children were treated in the same way.

The dead body was left swinging for all to see and to remind African-Americans that they were not truly free. During the early twentieth century and well into the twenties, lynchings were a constant threat and The National Association for the Advancement of Colored People (NAACP) was formed to combat this problem.

In the twenties, second-class status and lack of opportunity were facts of life for African-Americans. They seemed to be standing still. Approximately 90 percent of African-Americans lived in southern states, and they were suffering. They viewed the North as a promised land. They believed dignity, opportunity, and freedom could be found there. Often late at night they packed whatever they could carry and ran away from the land that was holding them against their will.

The period from 1915 to 1940, when African-Americans migrated north en masse, was called "The Great Migration." Up North they looked for freedom, opportunity, and the excitement of city life. What they found was another form of racism, but at least they could make a decent living and feed their families.

Harlem was the number-one destination and was considered "the black capital of the world." Madame C.J. Walker, a former washer woman, became the first African-American millionaire when she invented the straightening comb and other hair care products. During the 1920s, Harlem's writers, artists, and musicians produced a large body of work inspired by their roots. "The Harlem Renaissance," "Negritude," and "Black Nationalism" were movements that shaped the cultural and political mood for this world-famous community.

Famous writers of the Harlem Renaissance were James Weldon Johnson who wrote the Negro National Anthem, "Lift Every Voice and Sing." Jean Toomer, Countee Cullen, Langston Hughes, Claude McKay, and Zora Neale Hurston wrote of Africa and their people and abandoned the practice of imitating white styles and themes. Downtown white patrons like Carl Van Vechten applauded their talent and provided financial support.

Harlem Renaissance writers were invited to Van Vechten's literary salons to discuss their work. Van Vechten wrote the novel *Nigger Heaven* and the title alone caused outrage in some circles and amusement in others. Many rich whites ventured to Harlem to see bandleader Duke Ellington at the Cotton Club, one of the most famous nightclubs in the country. Each year there was a black play on Broadway.

In the twenties, political activist Marcus Garvey planted the first seeds of the black power movement with his motto "Up You Mighty Race." His "Back to Africa" movement won the support of followers nationally because African-Americans were tired of being beaten down. Garveyites dressed in military uniforms and paraded in proud pagaentry through the streets of Harlem.

In 1926 scholar and historian Carter G. Woodson initiated Negro History Week. The week focused on the achievements of Negroes past and present. He also published the *Journal of Negro History* and formed the Association for the Study of Negro Life and History.

Whites and blacks joined together to form The National Association for the Advancement of Colored People (NAACP), to deal with the problem of lynchings. Scholar W.E.B. DuBois became one of the first founders of the NAACP and edited the organization's *Crisis* magazine. *Crisis* became both a literary and political vehicle for African-Americans at the time.

Around the same time, a new music was born in New Orleans, Louisiana. Jass, as it was first called, was a hot, driving sound. At first considered merely race music popular among blacks, jazz could be heard from New Orleans to Kansas City to Chicago to New York and soon became American music. It is said that jazz "completely transformed the popular music of the country." (Hoff Wilson, p. xxiii). Kid Ory, King Oliver, and trumpeter Louis Armstrong were some of the early jazz talents. Some music historians credit jazz as the first music to be created in America for classical music was borrowed from Europe.

Another nickname for the twenties in the United States was the Jazz Age. Jazz was more than music; it was a rebellion. The music had a rhythm, emotion, and free form that fit in with the fast paced changes of the decade. Jazz was a way of life that went beyond entertainment to culture.

However alive and exciting urban living might have been at this time, many southern-born African-Americans found it uncomfortably different from the rhythm of rural life. Many suffered loneliness and destruction. Others found themselves involved in the betrayal of values and customs they once held dear.

Fon W. Boardman in his book *America and the Jazz Age* sums up the decade. "Life in the United States was made up of all these things—lynchings and refrigerators, short skirts and votes for women—and many more." To some it seemed like the best of times, to others it seemed a barren era, morally and intellectually. Morrison weaves her story over, around, and through the black experience at this time.

Master List of Characters

Narrator—*unnamed. Moves in and out of the story.*

Violet Trace—*The main character, a hairdresser. She has been married to Joe Trace for 20 years. She has trouble holding on to her husband and her sanity. When her husband shoots his lover, Violet is thrown out of the funeral for trying to disfigure the corpse's face.*

Joe Trace—*A main character, the husband of Violet, a cosmetics salesman. He has named himself Trace because he can find no trace of his mother.*

Dorcas Manfred—*The 18-year-old girl that Joe falls in love with. She is being raised by her aunt Alice Manfred because her parents were killed in racial incidents. Her only interest is to explore her sexuality.*

Wild—*Joe Trace's mother. She could not speak and lived almost like an animal in the cane fields. Joe was hurt that she could never care for him or acknowledge him as a child.*

Golden Gray—*A white-skinned man whose blood is half black. He* *is named for the color of his eyes. As a child, he was cared for by Violet's grandmother, True Belle. His mother is Vera Louise Gray and his father is Henry Lestory. When he finds out his father is black, he vows to kill him.*

Rose Dear—*Violet Trace's mother. The pressures of trying to provide for her children lead her to commit suicide by throwing herself down a well.*

True Belle—*Violet's grandmother, Rose Dear's mother. She comes to the rescue of the family when they are penniless. She also raised Joe's father, Golden Gray*

Alice Manfred—*Dorcas' aunt who is eager to care for her sister's child. She is considered well-to-do in Harlem society. She wants Dorcas to be above the average street people, so she raises her with an iron hand.*

Malvonne—*Joe and Violet's upstairs neighbor. She has allowed Joe and Dorcas to meet secretly in her apartment and feels guilty about it.*

Sweetness—*Malvonne's no good nephew. She has raised him as her own son. He is a very minor character who steals the neighborhood mail looking for money.*

The Miller Sisters—*Francis and Neola. They care for Dorcas as a child and preach about the sins of sex.*

Violet's father (unnamed)—*Husband of Rose Dear. He is always away from home when the family needs him. When he returns he brings money and trinkets for everyone.*

Stuck and Gistad—*Joe's two buddies. They don't always tell him about Violet's crazy behavior.*

Hunter's Hunter—*(This is a name given periodically to a man who is a good woodsman.) A man who teaches Joe and Victory about the woods. Also the name used for Henry Lestory, Golden Gray's black father.*

Henry Lestory—*An ex-slave who was Golden Gray's father. He was also called Hunter's Hunter.*

Vera Louise Gray—*Golden Gray's mother. Her child was fathered* by a black slave and as a result, she was banished from her home. Her father owned the plantation where True Belle was born. She took True Bell with her when she was sent away to Baltimore.

Colonel Wordsworth Gray—*Vera Louise's father, Golden Gray's grandfather. He owned a plantation in the area. He disowned his daughter when he discovered a slave was the father of her child.*

Honor—*A local teen who helps Henry Lestory around the farm.*

Victory Williams—*Joe's childhood friend. He always has the answers Joe needs.*

Rhoda and Frank Williams—*Victory's parents. They raised Joe as if he were one of their own children.*

Acton—*Dorcas' new, younger boyfriend.*

Felice—*Dorcas' best friend, raised by her grandmother because her parents are live-in servants in upstate New York. She becomes friends with Joe and Violet.*

Summary of the Novel

Jazz is the story of a husband and wife living in Harlem, New York in the 1920s. Joe and Violet Trace's marriage has experienced the usual ups and downs, but in the winter of 1926, their lives are nearly destroyed by Joe's infidelity with 18-year-old Dorcas whom he shoots to death. Because there are no witnesses, Joe is not arrested or made to pay for his crime in the traditional sense. Instead, he punishes himself.

His wife Violet is humiliated and outraged by Joe's betrayal of their love. Her reaction is to blame the dead girl and to strike out against her. Violet attends Dorcas' funeral to see what makes this girl so beautiful and why her husband loves her so fiercely.

At the funeral, Violet tries to attack the corpse with a knife. Violet is physically thrown from the funeral service. Now both Joe and Violet are the subjects of ridicule in their community.

However, neither of them is concerned. Joe is too busy crying. Violet spends her days trying to find out more about her husband's dead lover. Violet still considers Dorcas her rival for Joe's affections.

Violet becomes more and more mentally unglued. She is willing to do anything to hold on to her husband and to keep herself from going crazy. Violet becomes friends with the dead girl's aunt Alice Manfred and with Dorcas' best friend Felice.

As the story unfolds, we find out what causes the anguish suffered by Joe and Violet. Joe wanted recognition from a mother who was unable to give it to him. Violet is haunted by her mother's suicide. Her mother threw herself down a well when the burden of having no money to care for her five children became too much.

These private agonies eventually cause the couple to pull away from each other. Joe's involvement with Dorcas broadens the barrier between them. By the time spring comes, the couple have forgiven each other.

Around this time Dorcas' best friend, Felice, becomes their friend and helps them return their lives to normal. From the beginning of the novel, the reader is led to believe that Joe shot Dorcas dead. But in the final pages Felice reveals some missing details, details that help the couple figure out what Dorcas was really like and how much responsibility Joe should take for his part in ending her life.

Estimated Reading Time

The novel *Jazz* is not divided into chapters, but stops and starts in short, unnamed and unnumbered parts. Extra time will be needed to get used to the rhythm and style of the writing. Many sentences need to be reread because they are long and have a complex construction. Other sentences need to be reread because they are beautiful examples of Morrison's way with words.

The reading should be divided into the following parts and time slots:

Parts 1 & 2	$1 \frac{1}{2}$ hours
Part 3	1 hour
Part 4	45 minutes
Part 5	1 hour
Parts 6 & 7	45 minutes
Part 8	45 minutes
Part 9	15 minutes

Upon finishing the book, spend another ten minutes rereading the first paragraph of Part 1. Your total reading time for this book is approximately six hours.

SECTION TWO

Jazz

Part 1

New Characters:

Narrator: *unnamed*

Violet Trace: *Joe's wife of 20 years. She is starting to lose her mind*

Joe Trace: *The husband of Violet. He has an affair with 18-year-old Dorcas*

Dorcas Manfred: *Joe's 18-year-old girlfriend who is eager to explore her sexuality*

Alice Manfred: *Dorcas' aunt. She cares for Dorcas when her parents are killed*

Malvonne: *Joe and Violet's upstairs neighbor. She feels guilty about allowing Joe and Dorcas to meet in her apartment*

Gistan and Stuck: *Joe's two best friends. Their names are always mentioned in the same breath*

Summary

Very quickly the narrator lays out the story of Violet's and Joe's scandalous behavior. Joe shoots his 18-year-old lover, Dorcas. His wife Violet's first reaction is to make a scene at the dead girl's fu-

neral. Violet is physically thrown out of the funeral service for trying to cut the dead girl's face with a knife.

Violet vows to get even with her husband. But first she frees
the pet birds that she loves so dearly and that love her in return. As
part of her plot to punish her husband for his misdeeds, she comes
up with two plans: to take up with a new boyfriend and to find out
more about her competition.

She focuses on the second. Violet is driven to find all she can
about the dead girl. She must know what Dorcas looked like, how
she did her hair, and what music she enjoyed. Violet practices danc-
ing in just the same way that Dorcas danced.

When the dead girl's aunt gives Violet a picture of Dorcas, Violet brings it home to rest on her mantelpiece. Joe and Violet stare
at the photograph at different times of the day for different reasons: Joe to ease his guilt and help himself remember the love they
shared; Violet to see through the girl's youth and beauty to find a
sneaky, husband stealer.

All this activity, the investigations, and doubling her workload
because Joe is too broken-hearted to work, is exhausting for Violet. She does not feel in control of her thoughts. Her mind has been
slipping away little by little for quite some time. Two incidents prove
that she is becoming more and more crazy. One time she sits in
the middle of traffic; another time, she almost steals someone's
baby. This part of the book ends with Violet remembering the days
when she had a good, strong mind.

Analysis

As the novel begins, it seems as if we are eavesdropping on a
conversation. Using a gossipy tone, the narrator first utters not a
word, but a sound— "Sth." "Sth" is the noise that is made when
you suck your teeth in response to something said.

The very first paragraph gives all the juicy details about what
happened to Joe and Violet. The rest of the novel then unfolds in a
very nontraditional way through fragments and flashbacks. Instead
of chapters, there are natural breaks in the narrative. The story is
told in bits and pieces that don't always seem to fit together. The
story doesn't go back to the past and steadily work its way up to
the present.

The narration is also unique. The narrator, who has no name, goes back in time, comes back to the present, and sometimes jumps back and forth. The narrator can also jump in and out of the story, or into the middle of someone else's story.

Jazz also makes full use of the magnetism of New York City. Sometimes city life explains the characters' behavior, sometimes city life causes it. The music of the era helps to set the scene. Another nickname for the 1920s is "The Jazz Age," a time when jazz was new and everyone wanted to be a part of it.

Morrison's writing is very poetic, full of similes that enrich her character descriptions. For example, she describes Dorcas' coloring as a "...cream-at-the-top-of-the-milkpail face." To describe older people she writes, "If they reach that, or get very old, they sit around looking at goings-on as though it were a five-cent triple feature on Saturday."

Morrison uses simile again when she contrasts the liveliness on the streets with the atmosphere at Joe and Violet's place. "But up there on Lenox, in Violet and Joe Trace's apartment, the rooms are like the empty birdcages wrapped in cloth."

Violet is 50 years old. Morrison makes use of simile again to describe how ridiculous she looks trying to dance in the same way as 18-year-old Dorcas. "It was like watching an old street pigeon pecking the crust of a sardine sandwich the cats left behind."

Following and understanding *Jazz*'s storyline is like trying to appreciate a long, twisting, turning solo by a jazz musician. The reader must listen closely to hear what Morrison is trying to say. The narrator will eventually lead the way, but close attention must be paid.

Study Questions

1. Why is Violet referred to as the "Bird Lady"?

2. Why does the narrator describe Joe and Dorcas' relationship as "one of those deep down, spooky loves"?

3. Why does Dorcas' aunt Alice refuse to turn Joe over to the police?

4. Compare and contrast Violet with Dorcas.

5. How does Violet respond to the shooting?

6. What are Joe's feelings about shooting Dorcas?

7. What is Violet's plan?

8. Describe the atmosphere in Joe and Violet's apartment.

9. Both Joe and Violet are in the beauty business. Explain.

10. Describe some of the things Harlemites are proud of in their community.

Answers

1. Violet is called the "Bird Lady" because she keeps a parrot and lots of other birds in her apartment. She communicates with the birds and her parrot says "I love you."

2. Joe and Dorcas' relationship is labeled "spooky" because it was unusual and unnatural. There was more than a 30 year difference in their ages. After Joe shot Dorcas he cried everyday about it and was unable to resume a normal life. To protect him, Dorcas refused to name Joe as the person who shot her. After her death, the love continued and became more intense.

3. Alice Manfred doesn't want the police involved because the police have traditionally been an enemy of the African-American community. The police are considered as dangerous as the criminals. She doesn't want them in her house sitting in her chairs. Furthermore, she has heard of Joe's tears and knows that he will punish himself.

4. Violet is attractive but very dark-skinned. She is 50 years old, has hard edges to her personality, and is starting to act crazy. Violet no longer talks to Joe because she has time only for her birds. Violet is very thin, yet very strong, and Dorcas on the other hand is very light-skinned with long hair. These are two pluses. She is not particularly attractive, but she is 18-years-old. Dorcas is feeling the full impact of her sexuality and is eager for intimacy. It is easy for Dorcas and Joe to share their deepest secrets. Violet is independant, but Dorcas is extremely vulnerable and needs Joe's protection.

5. Violet responds to the shooting by totally losing her mind. She is angry and wants revenge so she tries to disfigure Dorcas' face at the funeral.

6. Joe grieves deeply for Dorcas. We assume he is sorry for what he has done because he cries constantly. He doesn't go to work anymore, nor does he speak. All he does is cry.

7. Once she was thrown out of the funeral, Violet still feels the need to get revenge. She plans to make Joe jealous, but that doesn't work so she decides to find out all she can about the dead girl.

8. Joe and Violet's apartment is lifeless. Empty bird cages fill the living room. Tears, anger, and sorrow permeate the rooms like a sickness.

9. Violet is an unlicensed beautician. She does hair in the kitchen of her apartment or when forced to, makes house calls. In addition to his job at the hotel, Joe sells Cleopatra beauty products door to door.

10. In Harlem in the 1920s residents are proud when the A&P supermarket hires its first African-American clerk. Harlemites are also proud of the African-American surgeon visiting Harlem Hospital and the 35 African-American nurses that have graduated from Bellevue Hospital. They flock to the parades in honor of the 369th Regiment and the Universal Negro Improvement Association led by Marcus Garvey.

Suggested Essay Topics

1. Violet was not always crazy. Compare and contrast Violet as a young woman with how she behaves in the beginning of the novel.

2. The New York City setting plays an important role in the novel. Choose two characters and discuss the impact the city has on their lives.

3. Alice Manfred gives Violet a photograph of her niece Dorcas. In your opinion, does placing the photo on the mantlepiece make the situation better or worse?

Part 2

New Characters:

Sheila: *One of Joe's customers that he was making a delivery to*

Wild: *Joe's mother. She lived in the cane fields. She was incapable of loving and caring for him*

Sweetness (aka William Younger): *Malvonne's nephew. He stole mail to look for money*

Summary

After the funeral, Violet lets her birds go. Her birds are the only creatures she can speak to and they speak back to her. Yet without the responsibility of caring for the birds, Violet finds herself without routine to her life. Now that they are gone, not caring for them causes her to have trouble sleeping.

Furthermore, Dorcas' memory casts a pall on the house. Like a sickness, Violet feels the pain of her memory everywhere. Joe on the other hand is thankful that Dorcas' memory is constant because he doesn't want to forget a single thing about her. Joe thinks back to how he met Dorcas while delivering beauty supplies. Joe remembers how she had given him signs that she was interested. He remembers the excitement of the desire he felt, and how he prepared for their coming together.

Joe fights to remember because he has already lost the memory of the love he and Violet once had for each other. That is why he needed Dorcas so that he could feel again.

Joe thinks back to how he and Violet met in 1906 in Vesper County, Virginia. Then he reminisces about how exciting it was coming to the city on the train. They took their time coming North and were part of the last wave of the Great Migration. Joe remembers that sometimes when African-American men needed jobs they were used as strike breakers.

Then Joe thinks about why people love the city so much. He remembers the city of Tyrell in Vesper County where he was born.

Joe wants to unburden himself from the hurts he suffered there. He still suffers about his mother and needs someone to talk to. Dorcas has lots of pain to share. She lost her mother and dolls to a fire and her father to a race riot.

Joe goes to his neighbor Malvonne to try to rent her room. The reader becomes aware that she has a problem with her nephew Sweetness. He steals letters to look for money and she reads them when she finds them. Malvonne intervenes when the letters call for some action. She is not interested in the lives of the important white people she works for. The letters and her community are what she cares about.

Joe convinces Malvonne to let him pay her to use her place for his meetings with Dorcas. Although he has never had an affair before, now Joe feels he needs somebody. Joe feels that Violet takes better care of her birds than him.

Analysis

If part one of the book explains what happens, this section of the book tries to explain why. This part looks at the character's feelings. How and why Joe got involved with Dorcas is explained. This explanation helps the reader to develop some sympathy for Joe because what he has done is so wrong. Telling his side of the story helps the reader to see why he thought the relationship was so right.

When Joe begins to share his past, his pain, and his history, we start to understand some of the reasons behind his actions. The reader begins to understand and sympathize with him just a little. A 50-year-old married man has no business getting involved with an 18-year-old, and he is totally incorrect for shooting her. When Joe cries and cries and suffers so, the reader begins to understand that he is not a classic villain but somewhat of a victim himself.

At this point in the novel, the characters search for peace and sleep and how to go on with their lives. In the hours they are not spending trying to figure out what happened, they try to rest.

Morrison uses simile to describe the end of the "Jim Crow" section of the train ride. The term "Jim Crow" refers to the laws and local customs that kept African-Americans separate and un-equal from whites. "Jim Crow" was used to describe discrimination in the South.

On the bus or riding a train, African-Americans had to use the back. They weren't served in most restaurants or allowed in the dining car of the train. Therefore, when they traveled, they would bring plenty to eat because no restaurant would serve them. They would sleep in their cars and go to the bathroom at the side of the road because they weren't welcome in southern hotels or restrooms.

This excerpt describes how the African-American attendants feel when the train passes through to the North and "Jim Crow" is no longer in effect. He wants the African-American passengers to take advantage of this new opportunity. "If only they would tuck those little boxes and baskets underneath the seat; close those paper bags, for once, put the bacon-stuffed biscuits back into the cloths they were wrapped in, and troop single file through the five cars ahead on into the dining car, where the table linen was at least as white as the sheets they dried on juniper bushes; where the napkins were folded with a crease as stiff as the ones they ironed for Sunday dinner; where the gravy was as smooth as their own, and the biscuits did not take second place to the bacon-stuffed ones they wrapped in cloth."

African-Americans loved the good that country life had to offer, but Morrison uses metaphor and personification to show the city has an attraction of its own. "Otherwise, if it wanted to, it could show me stars cut from the lamé gowns of chorus girls, or mirrored in the eyes of sweethearts furtive and happy under the pressure of a deep touchable sky. But that's not all a city sky can do. It can go purple and keep an orange heart so the clothes of the people on the streets glow like dance-hall costumes."

Study Questions

1. Why did Violet have trouble sleeping at night?

2. Why does Joe try so hard to remember everything about Dorcas?

3. How will these memories help Joe?

4. What are some of the reasons that African-Americans came to the city?

5. Why does Joe want to have the affair in the first place?

6. Where does Dorcas want Joe to take her?

7. How does Malvonne feel about the lives of the people she works for?

8. Explain what Malvonne tries to do with the letters.

9. How did Joe and Violet meet?

10. Could the city compete with the beauty of the country?

Answers

1. Violet has trouble sleeping once the birds are set free. Little things she had to do for them at night like covering their cages, helped her settle down to sleep.

2. Joe sits around and thinks about Dorcas day and night. He tries to remember everything beginning with the time he first met her. This way her memory won't fade and he can keep their love alive.

3. Remembering Dorcas and the intensity of his feelings for her will help him stay young. When he can't remember exactly how he felt at the time, he will be old.

4. African-Americans came North to find work opportunities. Another important reason was their search for rights and dignity. The South was strictly segregated and regarded them as second-class citizens.

5. Joe thinks about having an affair because Violet rarely talks at all these days. She only thinks and cares about her birds.

6. Dorcas wants Joe to take her to the club Mexico. She is tired of sneaking around and hates that their relationship has to be secret.

7. Although Malvonne cleans the offices of some very important people, she does not care about the pictures on their desks and the information she can find out about in their garbage cans. Malvonne is more concerned about her friends and neighbors in Harlem.

8. Malvonne discovers that her nephew has been stealing people's mail. He opens the letters looking for money. Malvonne reads the letters and feels bad that they will never get where they are supposed to go. She tries to intervene when she can.

9. Joe and Violet met when Joe fell out of the walnut tree he had been sleeping in.

10. Although the country has birds, streams, and beauty at every turn, the city also has a beauty to offer. In fact the city, a sculpture of stone on stone, can be more beautiful. The city sky at night, for example, can find no country rival.

Suggested Essay Topics

1. Was Joe and Dorcas' relationship doomed from the start?

2. Joe and Dorcas were able to share some very painful hurts with each other. Discuss the source of pain for each.

3. Describe the differences in the way Joe and Violet react to Dorcas' everpresent memory.

Part 3

New Characters:

Felice: *Dorcas' best friend*

The Miller Sisters: Frances and Neola: *They care for Dorcas and other neighborhood children while their mothers are working*

Summary

This section of the novel opens with a funeral parade in protest of the killings and riots in East St. Louis in July of 1917. Blacks march quietly but forcefully down 5th Avenue. Dorcas' parents were the victims of the racial attack and the protest is in their honor. Alice Manfred began caring for her sister's nine-year-old orphaned

child. Alice tries to find comfort from the tragedy in the beat of the drums and the looks on the marchers' faces.

The novel starts to unfold Alice Manfred's background. The fears and torments she has been wrestling with all her life are described. Now her sister and brother-in-law have died at the hand of racist whites. Another loss for her is that her husband left her for another woman.

As a teenager Alice Manfred was made to feel uncomfortable about the maturation of her body and the development of her sexuality. She received confusing signals from her restrictive parents. For example, her breasts were bound to hide them.

She tried to do almost the same thing with her niece Dorcas. Alice Manfred admits to the mistakes she made with Dorcas and runs them over and over in her head. Alice still asks herself again and again why the girl is dead.

Was she wrong to teach her to escape from the looks and propositions of white men? Her way to save Dorcas was to cover her up and dress her like a child. Alice Manfred required that Dorcas hide her hair under a hat and her developing body under dresses meant for a much younger girl.

Alice Manfred was afraid of how men reacted to her and how she was misjudged and mistreated because of the color of her skin. Alice was overprotective of Dorcas. She insisted that Dorcas hide herself and make every attempt to be invisible.

But Dorcas' mind and body fought against her aunt's rigid and unrealistic rules. Dorcas would sneak out to parties. She eagerly sought the very things her aunt was hiding from. Dorcas' body was looking for trouble. She felt a fire inside her body that was dying to be satisfied at any cost.

She sneaked out to a dance with her best friend Felice. Perhaps because of the way she dressed, the popular twins that she reached out to, rejected her. They dismissed her with just one look. This rejection was so devastating to Dorcas that it made her life seem unbearable.

This chapter also shows Joe's popularity with women. He has good looks, unusual eyes, and his old-time southern manners. His way with women was a necessity in his business, but he never let things get out of hand—until Dorcas.

We see how Joe and Dorcas meet. Ironically, Aunt Alice is present and her over-protectiveness has been in vain. Joe stops by to make a delivery and as he leaves, he whispers in Dorcas' ear.

We find that Aunt Alice feels women are "sitting ducks" for abuse of every sort. The only way she knows how to protect herself is to place herself under God's protection or to join a womens' club to form a sisterhood. Alice was a middle-class black woman and looked down on her own people who weren't on the same level. She didn't understand their ways or their music.

After Dorcas' death, Alice Manfred adds anger to her fear. As a result, she finds herself braver than she has ever been before. She is brave enough to finally allow Violet to visit her, after months of trying to get in to see her.

At first Alice and Violet didn't know what to do with each other, and they just talked in riddles to each other. Then Violet explains that she and Joe came to New York to make money. She tries to give Alice Manfred an idea of what kind of man Joe used to be. Finally, Violet admits, besides trying to find out more about Dorcas, she visits Alice to have a place to sit down and rest.

Alice notices Violet's craziness, but also notices that Violet is not harmful. The women start to bond. Alice accepts Violet and her ways and mends her clothes and makes her tea. Violet feels she owes Alice an explanation for her behavior. Violet asks her "Wouldn't you fight for your man?"

Alice is forced to answer no because when her husband ran off with another woman, she did absolutely nothing. The hurt and anger she felt is still bottled up inside. Alice is forced to admit that she still dreams of vicious revenge against the woman her husband ran away to.

Analysis

Dorcas was waiting for something to set her free from the unquenched fire inside her body. The city's music, full of vitality, seemed to present the way out. Morrison uses personification to show that the music has a voice and a mind of its own. "Alice Manfred had worked hard to privatize her niece, but she was no match for a City seeping music that begged and challenged each and every day. 'Come,' it said. 'Come and do wrong.'"

Morrison makes use of simile to allow Alice to describe how the music that is everywhere, rubs her the wrong way. The music was very sexual and Alice was alarmed by the way it touched memories deep inside her soul. In spite of themselves, women even older than she found themselves singing along in agreement.

"Songs that used to start in the head and fill the heart had dropped on down, down to places below the sash and the buckled belts. Lower and lower, until the music was so low-down you had to shut your windows and just suffer the summer sweat when the men in shirt-sleeves propped themselves in window frames or clustered on rooftops, in alleyways, on stoops, and in the apartments of relatives playing the low-down stuff that signaled Imminent Demise."

An excellent example of personification can be found in another description of the impact of the music. "And if that's not enough, doors to speakeasies stand ajar and in that cool dark place a clarinet coughs and clears its throat waiting for the woman to decide on the key."

Personification is used again when Alice blames music for the negative behavior of the rioting crowds, the music is described as having an appetite. "It's longing for the bash, the slit; a kind of careless hunger for a fight or a red ruby stickpin for a tie—either would do. It faked happiness, faked welcome, but it did not make her feel generous, this juke joint, barrel hooch, tonk house, music."

Soon after there is a reference to public signs. The reader should add commas to separate the thoughts that are just running together like they do in one's mind. This will help the paragraph to make more sense.

A continued conflict in the novel is Dorcas' sexual desire versus Aunt Alice's puritanical approach to childrearing. The intensity of the desire Dorcas feels propels her to go directly against her aunt's warnings. Dorcas' rejection by the twins at the party makes this need even more intense. She turns to Joe. The relationship between Dorcas and Joe might be described as a mid-life crisis that meets an adolescent crisis in a head-on collision.

Study Questions

1. What was the purpose of the protest march?

2. Alice Manfred made a good living. How did this affect her attitude about things?

3. How did Dorcas react to the tragedy surrounding her parents' deaths?

4. In your opinion what long-lasting effect did her parents' deaths have on Dorcas?

5. How did Alice and the Miller Sisters feel about the music?

6. Describe Dorcas' personality as a child.

7. What happened to Neola Miller's left hand and how did Dorcas react to the story?

8. To be funny, what did people change Violet's name to?

9. How did Dorcas describe her life as a 17-year-old?

10. What did the city whisper to Dorcas and to anyone who would listen?

Answers

1. Dorcas and her aunt attended the protest parade in honor of her parents who were killed in two separate racial incidents. African-Americans responded solemnly and in silence against such acts of violence that were occurring in locations throughout the country.

2. Alice Manfred would be described as bourgeois. She had made it and could not understand why everyone hadn't. She thought the average African-American was beneath her.

3. Dorcas' reaction to her parents' deaths was to become mute. For a long period of time she refused to speak.

4. Since she never really talked about her parents' deaths, she never really healed from the tragedy. The pain was still very much inside of her and affected her attitude about herself and life in general.

5. Alice Manfred and the Miller Sisters felt that the music everywhere in their community was the cause of all of African-Americans' problems. They felt the music was low-down

and dirty. Alice especially hated the music because it made her feel something inside even when she didn't want to.

6.   As a child, Dorcas was always bold.

7.   Like most women, Neola Miller wore her engagement ring on her left hand. This hand shriveled up when her love did not come for her.

8.   People jokingly called her Violent instead of Violet.

9.   When Dorcas is rejected by the handsome twins at the party, she feels her life is unbearable. Like most girls her age, one thing after another makes her feel she will never fit in, be accepted, or be fulfilled. Dorcas has no boyfriend and dresses like a baby. Her body longs for a love that she feels she will never find. She feels the situation is hopeless.

10.   The music and pulse of New York City whispers to Dorcas and anyone else who will listen, "Come. ... Come and do wrong."

Suggested Essay Topics

1.   Joe's affair with Dorcas was totally out of character. Describe the kind of man he normally was.

2.   The Miller Sisters preached fear and damnation to the children they cared for by using Bible stories. Dorcas, however, always missed the point and read something else into the stories. Explain.

3.   Alice Manfred's approach to childrearing was based on the way she was raised. What are some of the biggest mistakes she made in raising Dorcas?

Part 4

New Characters:

True Belle: *Violet's grandmother. She was taken away when a slave, to help her mistress in Baltimore. She returns to help her daughter and granddaughter when she hears they are in trouble*

Rose Dear: *Violet's mother. The strain of trying to single-handedly feed five children and the humiliation of being evicted cause her to eventually commit suicide*

Father: *Violet's father is unnamed. He left his family when he could no longer bear the hunger and hopelessness of the land. He would return periodically with presents for everyone*

Summary

In this part of the novel, we get a chance to go inside Violet's head and see what she is thinking and feeling. She feels like there is another person inside of her, seeing through her eyes and using her body. "That Violet," as Violet calls her, sees things Violet doesn't see and does things Violet would never think of doing.

It was "That Violet" that made the scene at the funeral. We find that the other Violet was also the one responsible for letting the parrot go. Every day the parrot said "I love you," when no one else did. Violet would never have let the parrot go.

Sitting in a drug store having a malted, Violet reflects on what Joe has done. It is hard for her to understand why. Violet needs more information and thinks of dozens of questions she could ask of Dorcas.

Violet becomes angry when she imagines things Joe and Dorcas might have done together. Violet has been in love with Joe since she met him at age 17. Joe, asleep in a walnut tree, fell down beside Violet and they were inseparable ever since that first meeting. After all the sacrifices she made to be with him, "Why, why, why did he do this to me?" she asks herself.

Once Violet starts thinking back, she recalls the time in 1888, when she was 12 and her grandmother True Belle came from

Balitmore to care for Violet and her brothers and sisters. Violet's father had left his family, causing his wife Rose Dear to fend for herself and the children. Rose Dear eventually committed suicide by leaping into a well. Violet's father visits ocassionally and brings gifts for everyone.

As this portion of the novel ends, Violet talks about her baby hunger. She and Joe agreed that they never wanted children. Then she developed a need for a child that was so strong that she started losing her mind. Ironically, Violet notices that Dorcas was young enough to be her daughter.

Analysis

At this point in the novel, Violet is being introspective. She holds a series of conversations with herself to sort out exactly what has happened. Each day she feels herself losing a little part of what is important to her—Joe, her parrot, her hope for a child. Ultimately, she feels herself losing control.

She feels like there is another person in her body. She knows she wouldn't try to hurt anyone the way "That Violet" did at the funeral. "That Violet has a whole different approach to life that knocks people out of the way and sees in everything, a weapon or opportunity to fight back."

The real Violet is not like that. She feels like she has a prolonged case of temporary insanity. Yet before this part ends, she admits that both Violets are indeed her.

While Violet is sipping a malted, Morrison uses simile to help us visualize how relaxing this is for Violet. "There she could sit and watch the foam disappear, the scoops of ice cream lose their ridges, and turn to soft glistening balls, like soap bars left in a dishpan full of water."

In this portion of the novel there is also an example of the difficulty in following Morrison's style. Violet is half crazy and her mind and thoughts are rambling. She believes Joe might have taken Dorcas to a night club and she is jealous. To show just how her mind is out of control, Morrison uses a sentence that is so long that it contains 190 words. The reader will not get lost if they remember this is just Violet talking to herself.

Meeting and falling in love with Joe helped Violet to put her mother's death behind her. Previously, she did not want to be out of sight of the well because her mother's life was down there. Violet never stopped wanting to know what pushed her mother to take that jump.

Violet couldn't understand which indignity signified the last straw for her mother. If her mother chose to continue living after the white men tipped her out of the rocking chair, why did she end her life when things had improved? After what Joe had done, Violet felt she finally understood. She was at the same hopeless point in her life.

Study Questions

1. What is the major difference between the two Violets?
2. At the funeral, what was the job that the boy ushers had to do?
3. Why did Violet's mother jump into the well?
4. Why didn't Violet want to have children? Why didn't Joe want to have them?
5. What are some of the sacrifices Violet made to be close to Joe?
6. What are some the tales people told about the big city?
7. What advice does Alice Manfred give to Violet?
8. Why didn't Violet want to be like her mother?
9. Why did "That Violet" throw the parrot out?
10. At the end of this chapter, laughter seems to save the day. Explain.

Answers

1. The original Violet is unsure of herself and starting to lose her mind. The other Violet is mean and very clear about what she wants to do. The other Violet turned everything she looked at into a potential weapon. She pushed people and fought back when necessary.
2. The boys thought that they would be pallbearers and direct

mourners to their seats. When Violet tried to attack the body, their job was to use every ounce of their strength to stop her.

3. Everyone was surprised when Violet's mother committed suicide because the family's living conditions were starting to improve. She didn't end her life when her husband left her, or when the white men evicted her from her home and dumped her from the rocking chair. Perhaps, she took her life at this time because she thought her children were better off under True Belle's supervision.

4. Both Joe and Violet love children but Violet remembered the powerlessness her mother felt when she was unable to feed them. She didn't want to put herself in that situation. Joe probably didn't want children because his mother was a wild woman. If it wasn't for the kindness of neighbors, he would have been an orphan.

5. When Violet met Joe she was supposed to work temporarily on a cotton crop. She never returned home and got a job on a nearby farm to be close to him. Before she met Joe, Violet never did any heavy farm work. By the time they got married she was muscular and strong and had calloused hands and feet.

6. The tales they heard were that people could earn a lot of money. People bragged that you could make money opening doors, shining shoes, or just helping people. The hardest thing to believe was that there were streets full of African-Americans making money all day and having fun all night.

7. Alice Manfred advises Violet to forget about what has happened and continue loving Joe.

8. Violet did not want to end up like her mother. Especially the way her mother handled most problems. Her solution was to do nothing.

9. The other Violet threw the parrot out because she couldn't bear to hear it say "I love you."

10. Alice and Violet are having an intense conversation about

Dorcas and Joe. What they are discussing is no laughing matter. Then they notice that the iron has burned the shirt Alice was working on. Upon seeing this accident, they laugh loud and hard.

Suggested Essay Topics

1. In her 40s Violet experiences a mother hunger that contributes to her losing her mind. Explain.

2. Violet tries to sort out her feelings about her father. In your opinion should he be criticized or admired for his approach to life?

3. Violet seems to both fear and admire the other Violet. Explain.

Part 5

New Characters:

Victory Williams: *Joe's childhood friend. They were raised as brothers and both were excellent woodsmen*

Rhoda and Frank Williams: *Victory's guardians. They treated Joe as if he were their own son*

Hunter's Hunter: *A skilled outdoorsman who taught Joe and Victory the ways of the woods*

Summary

Spring has come to the city. The narrator begins by making observations about the community waking up from the hibernation of the winter of 1926. In addition to all of the physical and psychological changes the spring will bring, the community looks for signs of change in Joe and Violet. Everyone is tired of waiting to see what revenge Violet will seek or if Joe will ever stop crying.

The narrator admits to being suspicious of Joe from the beginning and feels that he has gone through a mid-life crisis of sorts. "Look out for a faithful man near fifty. Because he has never messed with another woman; because he selected that young girl to love, he thinks he is free. Not free to break loaves or feed the world on a fish. Nor to raise the war dead, but free to do something wild."

The narrator understands that although Joe is 50 years old, he feels 16 inside. Why didn't he talk about Dorcas to his friends? Why didn't he get some advice or help?

Joe tells his side of the story. He tries to explain that Dorcas was like candy to him. Dorcas made him feel fresh and new and made him change himself. He was content to stay put in the place where he was born, but circumstances caused him to successfully change himself seven times before. But the change he made for Dorcas, was one change too many.

The first time Joe changed himself was when he named himself. He gave himself the last name Trace because there was no trace of his real parents. The second change he made was when he was trained to be a man by Hunter's Hunter.

Joe changed again when he was forced to leave his hometown of Vienna when a fire burned out all the fields and homes. He walked 15 miles to find work and he met Violet there. The fourth time Joe changed was when he finally decided to move up North.

The fifth change for Joe took place when he and Violet moved uptown to Harlem. There they lived in a large, well-kept apartment building. Joe changed again for the sixth time when he was nearly killed during a race riot. He was hit in the head with a pipe and being that close to death always changes a man.

Joe changed the seventh time because he thought people would change their minds about racial inequality. Black troops fought so valiantly in World War I that he foolishly believed they could expect democracy at home.

Joe sums up the impact of the changes he has made in his life. "I changed once too often. Made myself new one time too many. You could say I've been a new Negro all my life. But all I lived through, all I seen, and not one of those changes prepared me for her. For Dorcas."

Joe continues to explain his background as a woodsman, a sharecropper and what brought him North. Joe was very impressed that African-American spokesperson Booker T. Washington was invited to the White House. He took that as a sign that it was time to move on.

He explained how he and Violet advanced from one job to another once they got to the city. She started as a live-in maid and he did everything and anything until he settled into hotel work. Whatever work Joe did up North was not half as hard as the work he was accustomed to doing in the fields.

Joe recalled the race riots of 1917 and how he was lucky he wasn't beat to death. Joe had a good job and felt that he had it made. He had a taste of American prosperity although on a different level. Then Violet started losing her mind.

When Dorcas meets, and is accepted by, a man her own age, she tries to breakup with Joe. He was hurt by the things Dorcas said to make him leave her alone. Joe finds himself unable to compete with the young flashy men that he called roosters or "Sweetbacks."

When things were going good in their relationship, what Joe liked most about Dorcas was her complexion. Some would say she had bad skin, but to Joe the marks on her face looked like animal tracks. The marks were shaped like little animal footprints and this reminded Joe of the woods he felt so comfortable in during his childhood. As a young man he was trained to follow the ways of the woods by Hunter's Hunter. Another lesson Joe learned was that white people showed kindness only to that which they pitied

More than anything else Joe was a woodsman and he knew that every creature leaves tracks. Joe had tracked his mother successfully and decided to track Dorcas in the same way.

Analysis

Spring traditionally means rebirth. For many, spring brings hope and signals the end of a winter of discontent. We have reached a turning point in the novel. The narration for the first time expresses several personal insights about Violet and Joe. The first person pronoun becomes a prominent feature of the narrator's voice.

The rest of this part of the novel shifts to Joe's voice as he discusses first his past with Victory and Violet, and then the onset of his affair with Dorcas. Joe fills the reader in on the story of his life; he refers to many important historical realities that need explanation. For example, when Joe and Violet were first married, they worked on someone else's land. This was called sharecropping and unlike most African-Americans, they were able to work their way out of their debts to head to the North.

Just as immigrants dreaming of coming to America believed the streets were paved with gold, African-Americans believed the North was the promised land. The North was an improvement, yes, but not quite a promised land. Race riots were common. Usually Northern whites were angry about the influx of African-Americans competing for jobs. African-Americans were angry about living and social conditions.

Scores of race riots occurred each year in response to lynchings, burnings, and mob violence. African-Americans fought back. One of the bloodiest race riots in American history took place on July 2, 1917 in East St. Louis, Illinois. Whites fought against blacks and hundreds were killed. Weeks later the NAACP organized 10,000 protestors in a silent march down Fifth Avenue in New York City.

In the novel Joe was hit in the head during a race riot, while trying to help a fallen child. Dorcas lost both of her parents to racial violence. Alice Manfred brings Dorcas back to New York, and one of the first things they do together is watch the dark and silent faces of the people who march in the protest parade.

Another issue that needs clarification is the series of names that African-Americans have used to identify themselves. At first African-Americans were called Colored or Negro. The word nigger is a purposeful mispronunciation of the word Negro and is viewed as a hateful racial slur.

During the sixties African-Americans wanted to name themselves and preferred to be called Black. The slogan "Black is Beautiful" tried to undo some of the negative images attached to the color of African-American skin. The name was changed again to Afro-American and finally to the current designation African-American. As a race of people, African-Americans have continued to struggle for the right to name themselves, and to arrive at a name that truly reflects their cultural heritage.

When African-Americans arrived in New York, they did not

start out in Harlem, which has become the African-American capital of the world. They lived in lower Manhattan, Greenwich Village, in the area of the 30s and later in the area of the 60s which was called San Juan Hill. African-Americans kept moving further and further uptown in Manhattan in search of better living conditions. Harlem was the last stop, and this is still an African-American enclave.

The 369th Regiment of the 93rd Division, was an African-American combat unit that fought in WWI. The following quotation comes from the book *Liberators, Fighting on Two Fronts in World War II:* "The 369th performed admirably in the fighting north of the Oise-Ardennes canal. It would be awarded more citations than any other regiment in the AEF. The first American unit to reach the Rhine River, the 369th fought for 191 consecutive days without losing a trench, giving an inch, or surrendering a prisoner." The French government awarded the entire unit its highest military honor, the Croix de Guerre.

Upon the 369th's return home, all of Harlem turned out for the parade in their honor. Now that they had proved themselves, the soldiers that returned home looked forward to full equality. However, the army and the country maintained their discrimination policies. Many soldiers who were embraced in France received no medals or recognition in this country.

Booker T. Washington and W.E.B. Dubois were two spokesmen for the African-American community. Booker T. Washington was considered a moderate, politically. He pushed for vocational training and thought racial and social equality should not be the goals. "In all things that are purely social, we can be as separate as the fingers, yet, one as the hand, in all things essential to mutual progress." Washington preached patience and stressed hard work. He won a lot of white support. He became president of Tuskegee University in Alabama, a school that provided this type of education for African-Americans.

W.E.B. Dubois, on the other hand, was an intellectual that developed the concept of "The Talented Tenth." This meant that one in ten African-Americans was bright enough to lead the other nine to social and political equality. He felt that the vote, higher education, and equal rights were of the utmost importance. He was the first African-American to earn a Ph.D. from Harvard University.

The two leaders fought against each other. Booker T. Washington's invitation to the White House, where he was actually offered something to eat and treated hospitably, was viewed as a great sign of progress for African-American people.

When Joe describes what his life was like in the South, he gives an unusual explanation. "To be colored was to be the same everyday." This translates to there was no hope, no inspiration, no opportunity. All African-Americans had to look forward to was their day-to-day survival and the same routine of hard work. They could expect no difference, no change, no chance for anything better. Joe was lucky, however, because he got to change seven times. Each time the change was far better until the last time.

In her description of the beauty of the spring day, Morrison makes use of simile in the following sentence. "After a light rain, when the leaves have come, tree limbs are like wet fingers playing in wooly green hair." Morrison also includes the lyrics to a song by a blind man making his way down the street. Joe thinks the song is about him.

> "Blues man. Black and bluesman. Black-there-fore
> blue man
> Everybody knows your name.
> Where-did-she-go-and-why man. So-lonesome-I-
> could-die man.
> Everybody knows your name."

Study Questions

1. The narrator feels that Joe should have gotten some advice concerning his affair with Dorcas. Why didn't Joe confide in his friends?

2. Why did Joe give himself the last name Trace?

3. What is a Hunter's Hunter?

4. Why does Violet begin to sleep with a doll?

5. On the outside Joe was 50 years old. What was he like on the inside?

6. Dorcas was like candy to Joe. What advice do our parents give us about candy?

7. What were some of the reasons for the race riots?

8. Why did Joe need Dorcas so badly?

9. What did ladies like about Joe?

10. What finally caused Joe to move to New York City?

Answers

1. Joe didn't confide in his friends because he felt they would laugh at him and be of no help. He also felt that he couldn't talk to anyone but Dorcas.

2. Joe named himself Trace because his parents disappeared without a trace.

3. Hunter's Hunter is a name of honor given to a woodsman with exceptional hunting, fishing, and tracking skills.

4. Although Violet said she didn't want children, reaching age 40 she starts to experience baby hunger. Sleeping with a doll satisfies this desire.

5. Although Joe was a middle-aged man, he felt like a 16-year-old inside. He was young at heart.

6. Parents always warn their children not to eat too much candy. Excess candy can ruin the teeth and cause a stomachache.

7. In the North, African-Americans and whites fought each other in the street over jobs, housing, and social indignities.

8. Joe was a 50-year-old man who felt that life was passing him by. At this point in their marriage, he and Violet rarely talked and he felt he needed to be actively loved again. Dorcas was the solution.

9. Ladies liked Joe because he was handsome, he was a gentleman, and he had a gentle, country way of speaking.

10. Joe felt it was time to move to the city once Booker T. Washington was invited to the White House.

Suggested Essay Topics

1. Discuss Joe's skills as a woodsman and how he put those skills to work in the city.

2. Joe felt he had good reason to be unfaithful to Violet. Do you agree or disagree?

3. Joe feels that the cause of the tragedy in his life is that he changed one time too many. Do you agree or disagree and why?

Part 6

New Characters:

Golden Gray: *The son of Vera Louise. He is raised as a white child by his mother and True Belle. At age 18 he is told his father is African-American*

Vera Louise Gray: *Golden Gray's mother. A white female that was ostracized by her parents for getting pregnant by a slave*

Colonel Wordsworth Gray: *Vera's father. He is outraged when he learns of his daughter's relationship with a slave. He gives her a suitcase full of money to start a new life elsewhere*

Mrs. Gray: *Vera's mother. What her daughter has done is so unacceptable that she turns her back on her forever*

Henry Lestory: *Golden Gray's father. He had a sexual relationship with Vera Louise when he was a slave on her father's plantation. He is known as Hunter's Hunter because of his skills as a woodsman*

Honor: *A teenage boy that does odd jobs for Henry Lestory*

Wildwoman: *The wildwoman that Golden Gray finds in the woods*

Summary

This section of the novel begins with the triumphant return of True Belle, Violet's grandmother. Twenty-two years earlier she left the county of her birth as a slave. When she got news of her daughter and grandchildren's living conditions, she came to the rescue. True Belle returned a free woman with her life's earnings sewed in the hem of her skirt.

As a slave, True Belle had no choice about leaving her family, but she was now free to make up her mind about coming back. Upon her return, she found her daughter and grandchildren so poor that she had to laugh to keep from crying.

True Belle puts their lives back in order. She also tells her grandchildren tales of her life in the big city. In Baltimore, her life was devoted to caring for her mistress and the child Golden Gray.

We learn that Golden Gray is the product of the love between Vera Louise Gray and one of her father's slaves. As a result, Vera is disowned by her parents. Such a child would normally be given up for adoption, but the child's white-like skin and golden coloring made him acceptable enough to keep.

The child becomes the center of attention for True Bell and Vera. He was well loved but never told the truth. He was never sure if Vera was his benefactor, his mother, or a kindly neighbor. At age 18 his mother tells him that his father was an ex-slave.

Golden Gray is devastated by this revelation. He is so angry that he vows to find and kill his father. To help, True Belle draws him a map. In his quest to find his father, Golden Gray encounters a wild and naked pregnant woman. The woman is injured in a storm. He refuses to look at her or give as much attention as he gives his horse.

Reluctantly, Golden Gray comes to her aid and takes her to Henry Lestory's house. There he waits for his father's arrival home. First, a teenage boy that does odd jobs for Henry Lestory arrives. He immediately tends to the unconscious woman. Once the wild women is cleaned the narrator points out that Wild has lips that could break someone's heart.

Analysis

Although this section of the novel starts off with True Belle and what her life has been like since she last saw her daughter, Golden Gray soon becomes the focus. We learn that Golden Gray is a product of the love between Vera Louise and a slave. This union is taboo on several different levels.

During slavery many white men took pride in fathering children with their female slaves. This act and the children that resulted increased their number of slaves and satisfied their sexual desires at the same time. However, a white woman that was sexually involved with a slave was thought to have committed an unforgivable sin. Yet both of these types of relationships occurred on a regular basis.

To be socially accepted and to distance themselves from the shame, white women traditionally gave these children up for adoption. We now live in an age of bi-racial marriages and multiculturalism. However, during the post-slavery period, miscegenation—marriage or sexual relations between the races—was against the law. Such laws stayed on the books well into the decade of the 1970s. Another important distinction was no matter how white someone looked, one drop of African-American blood made the person African-American.

Once Golden Gray found out his true parentage, he was in turmoil. Although he was rich and handsome, he knew that being classified as African-American would ruin his life. With the truth his mother finally told, he instantly went from being raised like the Prince of Wales, to being a second-class citizen.

Perhaps Golden Gray thought he could wipe out his African-American blood by killing his father. Golden Gray had many confused feelings at this time. Although he wanted to hate his father, he also wanted to love his father, as every child wants to love his father.

Golden Gray was further confused because True Belle was his first love. He looked upon her like a mother or a mammy, as she would have been called at the time. Slaves like True Belle and later live-in domestic workers were often forced to leave their own children at home unattended while they cared for white children. To compensate, these white children became the center of their lives.

When Golden Gray rescues the wild, naked, and pregnant coal-black women, he is at first repulsed. Then he thinks of his black horse that he loves. These thoughts make him able to touch her and help her. Meeting the wild woman the way he did makes Golden Gray confront his new racial identity right away. When he looks upon the girl as a human being, he is further confused by her beauty and the feelings she has stirred inside him.

Morrison continues to use masterful descriptions to give the reader a sense of place as Golden Gray sets out in search of his father. "Then without warning as the road enters a valley, the rain stops, and there is a white grease pat of a sun cooking up there in its sky." When he finally reaches his father's house, Morrison uses metaphor to help you picture what the space looks like. "Certainly the owner never expected a horse and carriage to arrive—the fence gate is wide enough for a stout woman but no more."

At his father's cabin, Golden Gray looks around and Morrison completes the picture by interjecting a sense of smell. "The odor of the invisible animals accentuated in the heat, mixing now with out-of-control mint, and something fruity needing to be picked." When Golden Gray brings the wild woman inside the cabin and forces himself to look at her, this metaphor gives us an idea of what he observes. "Darker than the blood though are her lips, thick enough to laugh at and to break his heart."

While Golden Gray waits for his father's return to the cabin, he has a conversation with himself. During this soliloquy, Morrison once again uses the image of the arm that shrivels due to the loss of love. Neola Miller, one of Dorcas' babysitters, lost the use of her left hand. Her engagement ring was placed on this hand and it shriveled up and became useless when her true love failed to return for her.

For Golden Gray, being without his father is like having his arm ripped from his body. Therefore, a part of him wants to accept his father so that he can feel complete. Golden Gray talks very passionately to himself in order to sort out his feelings.

Golden Gray's mother, Vera Louise, was considered a suffragette by Baltimore society. A suffragette was a women who adamantly advocated the right of women to vote. "The Women's Suffrage Movement" won the right to vote in 1920 via the Nineteenth Amendment to the Constitution.

Study Questions

1. Describe what Violet's life was like at age 12.

2. Why do you think Violet's neighbors were so generous in their help to her family?

3. Why did Violet's father leave the family?

4. What was True Belle's reaction to Golden Gray's beauty?

5. Why was Golden Gray referred to as an orphan?

6. What would Vera Louise have done with the child if he did not look so blond?

7. Describe the environment in which Golden Gray was raised?

8. Describe Colonel Gray's reaction and Mrs. Gray's reaction to Vera Louise's pregnancy.

9. True Belle was a slave and had little choice about going to Baltimore with her mistress. Discuss the family True Belle left behind.

10. How much pay did True Belle get for 22 years of work?

Answers

1. At age 12, after her father deserted his family, Violet lived in poverty with her mother and four brothers and sisters. They were evicted from their home and they were often hungry.

2. The neighbors were so helpful because they understood that the same thing could happen to them. They were just a bit luckier so they shared whatever they had.

3. Violet's father gave up and left. He was tired of the work, the hunger, and that he couldn't do anything about it.

4. As a baby, Golden Gray was so beautiful that every time True Belle looked at him she had to laugh.

5. Golden Gray was called an orphan because his mother did not want the community to know she was unwed with an illegitimate child. She certainly didn't want anyone to know her child's father was an ex-slave.

6. Golden Gray's coloring saved him from being abandoned in an orphanage. Because he was so light, his mother was able to keep him and let him pass for white.

7. Vera Louise was a rich woman, and she raised Golden Gray like a young prince. He received much love and attention from both Vera and True Belle.

8. Colonel Gray was horrified by the idea of Vera's relationship with a slave. He knocked her down and sent her away forever. Vera Louise's mother also turned her back on her.

9. True Belle was forced to leave her husband and two daughters behind to go with Vera Louise to Baltimore. True Belle asked her sister to watch out for her family. She didn't see her daughter Rose Dear again until she came to help her 22 years later.

10. True Belle had earned 10 eagle dollars for 22 years of work.

Suggested Essay Topics

1. Golden Gray becomes True Belle's whole life. Why?

2. When Golden Gray notices the wild woman on the road and helps her, the narrator calls him a hypocrite. Explain why and whether you agree or disagree.

3. To be dispossessed for nonpayment of rent meant that your furniture was put out of the house onto the street. This was a great humiliation for any family. Discuss the course of events that made Rose Dear's eviction worse than the usual humiliation families face in this situation.

Part 7

Summary

Golden Gray wonders what his reaction will be when the wild woman opens her eyes. Stories were told that Wild, so named by Hunter's Hunter, liked men with hair the same color as the golden corn fields. Wild lived in the cane fields. She was like a creature that could be as gentle as a deer or as fierce as a tiger.

There was something about her look, her touch, and her laugh that drove men crazy. Older men were particularly vulnerable because they saw her once in their youth and wanted to see her again. To others, her existence was more like a tall tale. According to local lore, the gaze of a wild woman could mark a man for the rest of his life. That is exactly what happened to Golden Gray.

Golden Gray finally has the conversation with his father that he has been waiting for. Their talk, however, turns out totally different than he has planned. Instead of the guilt, anger, and revenge Golden Gray expects, Henry Lestory easily diffuses the situation with a dose of tough love.

"Look here. What you want? I mean, now; what you want now? Want to stay here? You welcome. Want to chastise me? Throw it out your mind. I won't take a contrary word. You come in here, drink my liquor, rummage in my stuff and think you can cross-talk me just cause you call me Daddy? If she told you I was your daddy, then she told you more than she told me. Get a hold of yourself. A son ain't what a woman say. A son is what a man do. You want to act like you mine, then do it, else get the devil out my house."

Joe comes back into the story with memories of how he tracked the wild woman when he found out she was his mother. At the news, young Joe suffered emotions that ranged from shame, to denial, and finally to the desire for his mother's love. He found signs of her in the woods and in a cave where he also saw many of Golden Gray's possessions.

Before Joe was born, his Hunter's Hunter tried to care for Wild when he found her pregnant and in need of help. When Wild gave birth, she had no mothering instinct. She would not look at the

baby or touch it. Joe was this child, and he always suffered from the absence of his mother's love.

Joe wanted some acknowledgment from his mother. He prayed for a sign, or a sound. He hoped that she would at least stick her hand out of the bushes so that he could have something to hold on to. Joe tracked his mother once again when the cane fields were afire. He was concerned about her safety.

When Dorcas leaves Joe, his mind turns to Wild and Hunter's Hunter. These thoughts make him think about hunting again. This time, however, he goes hunting for Dorcas and her love.

Analysis

Many questions arise in this area of the story. References to the identity of Joe's mother, the relationship between Golden Gray, and the wild woman are issues that remain unclear. Much of what we can discern about these relationships are based on subtle clues or abstract references. Sorting it all out is difficult.

The wild woman in some way helped Golden Gray to overcome the urge to kill his father. How did she soothe his soul? Did Golden Gray experience the stirrings of a sexual attraction?

Something about the nature of their relationship is inevitable because Wild is always attracted to blond men with hair the color of sugar cane. What happened to Golden Gray? Why were his things in Wild's hiding place? Did he run off with Wild? We can wrestle with answers to these questions but depending upon interpretation, there is much room for debate.

What seems to be consistent, however, is that with every generation there is a new Hunter's Hunter and a new wild woman. The first Hunter's Hunter we meet, is the one that trains Joe. The next Hunter's Hunter we meet is Henry Lestory, Golden Gray's father.

Joe's Hunter's Hunter trained Joe well and his tips on animal behavior could be easily applied to human behavior and relationships. Hunter's Hunter explains this to Joe and Victory when they joke about catching Wild and killing her. "I taught both you all never kill the tender and nothing female if you can help it. Didn't think I had to teach you about people. Now, learn this: she ain't prey. You got to know the difference."

But Joe disregards this important lesson and begins to track

Dorcas down. Does Joe lose his mind a little too, just like the way Violet does? Dorcas is the first and only woman Joe has truly loved. Although he has developed a love for Violet, he married her only to replace his mother's love.

Is Joe ignorant of what will happen when he finally tracks Dorcas down? He is not thinking clearly and has lost his bearings. To find his way out of the pain he does something that is very natural—act like a woodsman.

Joe keeps chanting Hunter's Hunter's advice, not to hurt the young, the female, but the warning does not manage to stop him. While he is tracking Dorcas down, his mind races back and forth from his days as a youth, to his search for his mother, to Dorcas and her young, new boyfriend. Dorcas is wild like his mother. Maybe that's why he loves her so.

Joe is unrealistic about what Dorcas' reaction will be when he catches up to her. He thinks she will be the same girl that he fell in love with. He thinks she will want to love him again.

Study Questions

1. What rule of woodsman etiquette did Golden Gray break?
2. How did Wild's presence disturb the thoughts of everyone in the community?
3. What is the range of emotions Joe feels about his mother?
4. Describe Wild.
5. Finally Joe curses his mother. What are some of his feelings about the situation?
6. Why did Joe work so hard?
7. Describe Golden Gray's conversation with his father.
8. How was their meeting different from what Golden Gray had planned?
9. What is Golden Gray's reaction when Wild opens her eyes?
10. Why does Joe decide to track Dorcas?

Answers

1. Woodsmen were allowed to enter someone's home or shed

for shelter but they were never supposed to drink their liquor.

2. Cutting sugar cane was hard and dangerous work. When men thought of Wild they weren't concentrating on their work. Time could be a waste of time or someone could get hurt. Children were afraid of Wild and mothers-to-be prayed that the new baby would not be like her. New brides left food for her to eat.

3. Joe was shocked and embarrassed when Hunter's Hunter hinted that Wild was his mother. Then he was angry that she didn't care about him. After his initial reaction to the news, Joe became curious, and would track Wild to find out more about her. Finally, Joe developed a strong desire to have his mother acknowledge him in some way, but she never did.

4. Wild was very black and very beautiful. She didn't speak or have any social graces. She lived in the cane fields or in bushes or caves in the woods. When she came in contact with people, she usually bit them. She had a very intense gaze. When men worked in the fields, they could feel her eyes upon them.

5. Joe gives up trying to get his mother to acknowledge him. In a way, he would have been happy to have a prostitute or the most worthless woman in the world for his mother instead of Wild. He curses his mother because even animals have a natural instinct to love and care for their young. His anger makes him judge his mother worse than an animal.

6. People thought that Joe worked so hard because he was industrious or that he really loved money. The real reason was that he was trying to work until he was too tired to think about his mother.

7. Golden Gray feels he will have the upper hand in his conversation with his father. He is drunk, and because he has been raised as a white child, he naturally feels superior. Henry Lestory, however, was unaware of his birth and tells his son so. Using a no nonsense approach he tells Golden Gray he is welcome to stay or to go.

8. Golden Gray's original plan was to kill his father. After the meeting with his father, he was unsure of what to do, so he takes no action at all.

9. His initial repulsion at her nakedness and layers of dirt changes to an awareness of her as a woman.

10. Joe tracks Dorcas because he doesn't know what else to do. He needs to talk to her and be with her again, and hunting her is the only way he knows to find her.

Suggested Essay Topics

1. Golden Gray was unsure of his parentage. When he was told the truth about his mother and father, explain how his life was forever changed.

2. Describe the range of emotions Golden Gray felt concerning meeting his father for the first time.

3. In your opinion, why is it so important for Joe to receive acknowledgment from his mother?

Part 8

New Character:

Acton: *Dorcas' new boyfriend. He is young and cocky and quite sought after*

Summary

The opening of this section sets the scene for the shooting. On January 2, a cold, cold day of continued Happy New Year celebrations, Joe finally locates Dorcas. At this time Dorcas starts to tell her side of the story.

She didn't mean to hurt Joe's feelings, but he wouldn't let her go. Dorcas is proud of the progress she has made in her life. She has a new look, a new boyfriend, and a new personality. At last she

has everything she has always wanted. Yet she is aware that Joe is coming after her.

Joe walks through the party unnoticed and shoots Dorcas before she fully realizes what is going on. She has trouble speaking and hearing, but we are aware of the thoughts that run through her mind. We know that she is cold and that she is feeling sleepy. She doesn't say anything about the pain but notices her boyfriend is angry about the blood on his jacket.

It is a while before the partygoers discover her bleeding in the bedroom. "Who has done this to you?" they ask. Dorcas doesn't want to say, furthermore, her voice is too weak to be heard. It is easy to guess who shot her, but she protects Joe by never saying his name.

Analysis

At this point, the narrative unfolds at a faster pace. In previous sections, the narrator tells one story in the middle of another, or goes back 30 years and then jumps back to the present. The last chapters are very short and the story is taking a more direct course to the end.

The last bits of information and missing pieces of the puzzle are starting to fall into place. Each character's relationship to the other has become clear. Joe has successfully tracked Dorcas and shot her.

At this point we are almost ahead of the story because we know what will happen after this. We've already been to the funeral and have already witnessed Joe's grief and Violet's behavior.

Morrison makes use of simile and personification to describe the good time had by all at the post-New Year's Eve party. "The laughter is like pealing bells that don't need a hand to pull on the rope: it just goes on and on until you are weak with it. You can drink the safe gin if you like, or stick to beer, but you don't need either because a touch on the knee, accidental or on purpose, alerts the blood like a shot of pre-Pro bourbon or two fingers pinching our nipple. Your spirit lifts to the ceiling where it floats for a bit looking down with pleasure on the dressed-up nakedness below."

Morrison uses personification again to give an idea of the music. "The music bends, falls to its knees to embrace them all, encourage them all to live a little, why don't you?, since this is the *it* you've been looking for." Then she uses simile and metaphor to compare the party to war and its aftermath. "Anything that happens after this party breaks up is nothing. Everything is now. It's like war. Everyone is handsome, shining, just thinking about other people's blood. As though the red wash flying from veins, not theirs, is facial makeup patented for its glow."

Study Questions

1. Why is Dorcas so happy at this point in her life?
2. Listening to Dorcas' side of the story, do you agree that she doesn't seem so bad after all? Why?
3. How would you describe Dorcas' new boyfriend?
4. How does Acton control Dorcas?
5. What went wrong when Dorcas tried to break up with Joe?
6. How was what Joe found at the party different from what he expected?
7. What is the hostess' reaction to the shooting? Acton's reaction?
8. Why didn't Dorcas go to the hospital?
9. Why doesn't Dorcas tell on Joe?
10. What is the difference between Dorcas' relationship with Joe and with Acton?

Answers

1. Dorcas is happy because she is living the life that she has dreamed of. She has a handsome boyfriend that is close to her age and the envy of the other girls. Her hair, shoes, and make up are those of a stylish young woman. No longer does she have to stuff herself into little girl dresses.

2. Throughout the novel Dorcas has been portrayed as a thoughtless, selfish girl. Hearing her thoughts for the first time makes the reader see that she was not all bad.

3. Acton is self-centered and doesn't love Dorcas in the same

way that Joe did. He is aloof and criticizing and this seems to make her love him more.

4. Acton controls Dorcas by telling her what to say, what to do, and what to wear. She thinks this is helping her develop a personality.

5. Dorcas practiced exactly what she wanted to say to Joe to end the relationship. But the words didn't come out right. He was so insistent, that she had to take a harder line. She didn't plan on saying hurtful things.

6. Joe thought that Dorcas was still the little girl he loved. What he found was a Dorcas that didn't look like, or act like, the one he remembered.

7. The hostess of the party was concerned that her party was ruined. She didn't like all the blood messing up her house. Acton spent the whole time wiping the blood off of his jacket.

8. Dorcas insists that she is not hurt badly and tells everyone she just wants to rest for a while.

9. Dorcas didn't tell on Joe because she knew what she said had hurt him. She also appreciated him as her first love and the first person to accept and encourage her.

10. Joe did little things to please Dorcas, like giving her gifts and money. It is the opposite with her new boyfriend. Dorcas gives Acton gifts and money and focuses on pleasing him. Joe wanted her to focus on pleasing herself.

Suggested Essay Topics

1. Compare and contrast Joe and Acton's treatment of Dorcas.

2. When Joe set out to look for Dorcas, he didn't want to shoot her, he just wanted to talk to her. In your opinion, what went wrong?

3. In your opinion did Dorcas want to die? Why did she just lie there and bleed to death?

Part 9

New Characters:

Felice's mother and father: *Live in servants that worked upstate in Tuxedo, New York. Because of their jobs, they could rarely spend time with Felice*

Felice's grandmother: *She raised Felice in her parents' absence*

Summary

Spring has produced one of the most beautiful days of the year and Harlem responds to the weather. From the street corners to the roof tops, the music sounds glorious and adds another dimension to the spring fever that is rampant. We also find the environment slightly improved in the Trace household. Joe doesn't cry as much or as loudly. Violet seems to have gotten a grip on her sanity.

On this beautiful day, Felice pays a visit to Joe and Violet. Felice can't find the opal ring that she let Dorcas borrow and wonders if Joe has it. Once inside the apartment, Felice talks about herself and how her parents are retired domestics that spent a large part of their lives working in Tuxedo, New York. Felice complains that she rarely got a chance to be with them, and has figured out an approximate number of days that they have spent time together as a family.

Felice talks about herself and her friendship with Dorcas. They were best friends and she feels she knows Dorcas better than anyone else. For months Felice has wanted to tell Joe to stop shedding tears because she feels Dorcas wasn't worth it.

Because the couple seems so nice, Felice is happy to put an end to their anguish. "Dorcas let herself die!" Felice proclaims. She explains to Joe that when Dorcas was shot, it was only a shoulder wound. Dorcas refused to go to the hospital or to let anyone help her because all she wanted to do was sleep. As a result she bled to death unnecessarily.

Felice takes this opportunity to ask Violet why she messed up

Dorcas' funeral. Violet's response is a hard to understand answer, but Felice seems to understand anyway. Just as Joe understands that he is still responsible for Dorcas' death, but he feels better about it. In return, Joe tells Felice things about Dorcas, things that might help Felice understand that Dorcas wasn't so bad after all.

Analysis

Here we have the denouement of the novel. All of the problems are solved; all of the important questions are answered. The name Felice means happy, and the information Felice shares about Dorcas makes this a happy day for Joe. This is the day he is absolved of his sins.

Felice visited Joe and Violet with one intention in mind, but she likes the couple and how they relate to each other. The three become friends. Seeing Felice on the way in the building, Joe and Violet are afraid she will be another Dorcas. But by the end of the visit they have become like a family. Felice is the daughter they never had and Joe and Violet the parents that were too busy working.

When Felice talks about her friendship with Dorcas, and how unusual it was, she is referring to the differences in their color. Even today, the lightness or darkness of skin color may determine acceptance for African-Americans in this country. A popular rhyme at the time the novel takes place, gives an idea of what skin color could mean in terms of social status. "If you're light, you're alright, if you're brown stick around, if you're black stay back."

School kids taunted Felice and Dorcas by saying the friends looked like a fly in the buttermilk. Felice being the fly and Dorcas the buttermilk. Even Felice's grandmother did not understand the friendship simply because the girls were so different in color. Like colors usually associated with each other.

Morrison approaches the color issue head on by making most of the characters very light or very dark. She allows no middle ground. Morrison uses this same approach with Joe's mother Wild. Wild is attracted to men with hair the color of sugar cane. Joe's skin color and unusual eye color prove he is the product of a black and white union. Other times Morrison makes the look of couples like Vera Louise and Henry Lestory coal black with blond, making a striking visual contrast. White-skinned Golden Gray admits that his first love was dark-skinned True Belle.

The concept of change is also a re-occurring theme. Previously, Joe talked about changing himself seven times. Violet brings in the concept of change once again when she advises Felice to change the world before it changes her. Violet also tells Felice to get rid of the person inside of her that doesn't feel like she belongs there. Violet explains that she killed that other Violet, and what was left, was something she could recognize—herself.

Before Dorcas dies, she asks Felice to tell Joe about the apple. This is a sign that Dorcas really did care about him. Earlier in the novel, Joe talks about Adam and Eve in the Garden of Eden. Joe looked at this Bible story in another context. "I told you again that you were the reason Adam ate the apple and its core. That when he left Eden, he left a rich man. Not only did he have Eve, but he had the taste of the first apple in the world in his mouth for the rest of his life. The very first to know what it was like. To bite it, bite it down. Hear the crunch and let the red peeling break his heart." Joe is Dorcas' first love, and he is hers.

Joe makes two very significant statements at the end of this section of the novel. After they have enjoyed a nice visit with Felice, Joe announces "This place needs some birds." Then a little later he says, " . . . I best find me another job." He thanks Felice for the happiness that is her name, and for bringing to him the will to live again.

Study Questions

1. What did Dorcas always talk about?

2. Compare and contrast Dorcas and Felice.

3. Dorcas had trouble getting boyfriends. Why?

4. Why did Felice visit Joe and Violet?

5. Felice's father had some very strong opinions. What were they?

6. Why does Felice admire Violet and Mrs. Manfred?

7. What did Felice mean when she said Dorcas pushed men?

8. Why didn't Felice go to Dorcas' funeral?

9. How does Violet describe Dorcas?

10. What comments does Felice make about Joe's unusual eyes?

Answers

1. Dorcas always talked about how someone looked. She wanted to be involved with a really good looking man.

2. Dorcas and Felice looked totally different. Dorcas was light-skinned, with long hair. Felice was dark-skinned. Dorcas was more bold and assertive than Felice. Felice was allowed to do the normal things for a girl her age. Dorcas' aunt tried to stop her from growing up. Both girls were raised by older female relatives.

3. Dorcas had trouble getting boyfriends because she wasn't particularly attractive. Some might say her light skin and long hair would make her pretty, but, it didn't. The childish way she dressed and wore her hair didn't help matters. Another problem was when a young man was interested, Dorcas was always trying to push him to do things he didn't want to.

4. Felice visited Joe and Violet to find out about her ring. She also wanted to tell Joe that Dorcas wasn't worth crying over.

5. Felice's father was considered a race man. When he read about lynchings and injustice in the newspaper, he was very angry. He felt that injustice for African-Americans was an everyday occurrence. Her father mentions the discrimination in baseball as a good example of how whites were afraid to compete fairly with African-Americans.

6. Felice admires Violet and Alice Manfred because they worked and were independant. During this period most women married and depended upon their husbands for care and support. Felice wanted to be different.

7. Dorcas pushed men to prove their love for her. They had to save her or fight for her or do something dangerous to make her satisfied. Most men didn't want to be bothered.

8. Felice didn't go to the funeral because she was angry at Dorcas for letting herself die. Felice felt that if Dorcas was really her best friend she would have saved herself so that they could be together.

9. Violet describes Dorcas as ugly, inside and out.

10. Joe has unusual eyes; one is blue, the other green. Felice called his eyes "double eyes." She described them as a sad one so people could see inside of him and a clear one so he could see inside of people.

Suggested Essay Topics

1. Violet finally manages to get rid of that other Violet and as a result regains her sanity. What lesson does this experience teach her?

2. During this period lynchings, race riots, and beatings by the police were the fear of most African-American households. Some of these same problems persist today. What were the causes of the racial tension, then and now.

3. In this part of the novel Felice becomes a heroine of sorts. Explain.

Part 10

Summary

The narration ends just as it began—with a conversation. The topic of the conversation is pain. Pain in the narrator's life and pain in the lives of others. Here the narrator does some soul searching and admits having no purpose in life but to observe the lives of others.

The narrator is hurt and disappointed about being totally wrong about Joe and Violet, that something was missed that caused the wrong conclusion to be drawn about the outcome of their re-

lationship. The narrator jumped to the wrong conclusion about Joe, about Violet, and about what would happen when they met Felice. The narrator predicted that the Dorcas thing would happen all over again.

The narrator sees where the mistake was made. For example, when Joe cried constantly, it wasn't just for Dorcas. Now it is clear that he could have been crying for Violet, his mother, or the fact that he made one change too many.

As the novel comes to a close, we are given the last details about the characters. Alice Manfred has moved back to her hometown. Felice remains true to her resolve. Joe finds another job and gets close to Violet again. They drink malteds together, talk to each other, and care for Violet's new bird Violet. The novel ends with the narrator longing to have experienced such love.

Analysis

The narrator, not clearly male or female, criticizes himself or herself for being a misinformed gossip. Throughout the novel the sex and identity of the narrator remain a mystery.

Exactly who is the narrator? Is she a woman who knew Joe and Violet? A neighbor? A friend of Joe's? Perhaps the narrator is the consciousness of the the African-American experience—a shade of the character's past lives.

At this point, the narrator seems to be speaking for the entire community when admitting the wrong conclusions were drawn. For the duration of the winter, the neighborhood has watched and waited for news about what will happen with Violet and Joe. They go as far as making predictions about what crazy Violet will do. Yet no one predicted that they would solve their problems in their own way and continue to love each other.

In the end, Joe and Violet have found peace in their lives and cooled down the hot flames boiling inside them. They are in bed and thinking of buying a sky blue blanket with satin trim. "Violet doesn't care what color it is, so long as under their chins that avenue of no-question-about-it satin cools their lava."

Joe and Violet have come to the realization that they really need each other. Joe needs Violet to help erase the image of Dorcas' red blood and the red-winged birds that were a sign that his mother was nearby. Violet turns to Joe to forget the sight of the dark well her mother jumped into. In her mind, she changes the well to a bright pool of water containing her father's little treasures. Joe and Violet forget about everything else and worry only about themselves. That is more than enough to keep their lives happy and occupied.

All the way to the final chapter Morrison remains poetic. The following sentence, for example, uses onomatopoeia. "I wonder, do they know they are the sound of snapping fingers under the sycamores lining the street?" Describing Joe and Violet as they lie in bed, Morrison emphasizes their closeness using this simile. "Breathing and murmuring under covers both of them have washed and hung out on the line, in a bed they chose together and kept together never mind one leg was propped on a 1916 dictionary, and the mattress, curved like a preacher's palm asking for witnesses in His name's sake, enclosed them each and every night and muffled their whispering, old-time love."

Study Questions

1. What did the narrator think would happen?
2. What actually did happen?
3. Why did Joe cry so much?
4. When Joe was hunting Dorcas what was he really doing?
5. Why did Wild hide from everyone?
6. Why does Joe love the long distance eyes of the soap box speakers?
7. What were some of the good things about Joe's new job?
8. Exactly how has Joe and Violet's relationship improved?
9. What are some of the things Violet tries, to help the new bird get well?
10. Explain how life is easier for Joe and Violet.

Answers

1. The narrator thought that Violet would hurt or kill Joe. When

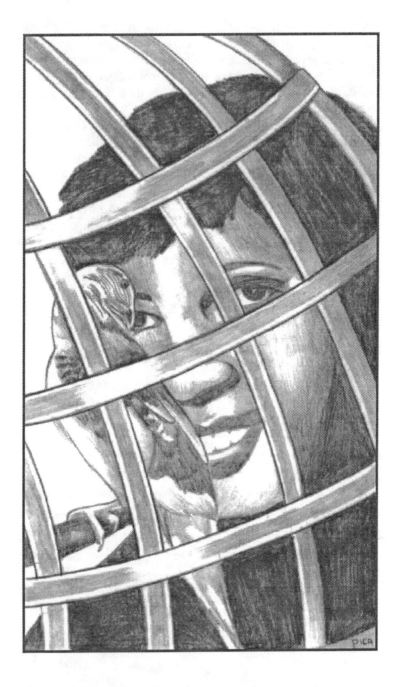

she saw Felice, she thought she would act just like Dorcas.

2. Violet and Joe saved their marriage and got their lives back in order.

3. Everyone thought Joe cried about shooting Dorcas. Now the narrator understands that he could have been crying for Violet, his mother, and for making one change too many.

4. The narrator believes that he might have been hunting for his mother at the same time.

5. Wild hid from everyone because she knew that she frightened people. She didn't want to scare anybody.

6. The long distance eyes of the soap box speakers reminds Joe of his mother's eyes.

7. Joe's new job required that he work at night. Now he was free during the day to spend time with Violet.

8. Joe and Violet's relationship has improved because they talk to each other and do things together like play cards. They appreciate each other and are in love again.

9. Violet's new bird is sickly. To make the bird get better she offers it special food, she talks sweet talk to the bird and finally lets the bird listen to music. The music helps the bird turn into a delightful pet.

10. Joe and Violet don't have to worry about the opinions or acceptance of anyone. Life is much easier for them now that they only have to worry about themselves.

Suggested Essay Topics

1. In your opinion, is the narrator male or female? Support your answer with examples from the novel.

2. Joe and Violet beat all the odds and stayed together. How do you think they managed to save the relationship?

3. The novel goes full circle when it ends with Violet caring for a new bird. Exactly how important is a pet to Joe and Violet's relationship?

Sample Analytical Paper Topics

The following topics provide an opportunity for you to analyze, synthesize, and evaluate what you have read. Each topic includes an outline that will serve as a guide and a starting point.

Topic #1

Although *Jazz* has many themes, the novel can be classified as a love story. Discuss the many different types of love explored in the book.

Outline

I. Thesis Statement: *The many different types of love portrayed in the novel include: the love between a man and a woman, mother love, love of country life, love of the city, love of music, and baby love.*

II. Love Between a Man and a Woman

    A. Joe and Violet

        1. Youthful years

        2. Mature years

    B. Joe and Dorcas

    C. Vera Louise and the slave

    D. Wild and Hunter's Hunter

III. Mother Love

    A.   Joe's love for Wild

    B.   Violet's love for Rose Dear

    C.   Vera's love for Golden Gray

    D.   True Belle's love for Golden Gray

IV. Love of Country Life

    A.   Joe and Victory

    B.   Hunter's Hunter

    C.   Wild

V.   Love of the City

    A.   Better than country life

    B.   Perfection

VI. Love of the Music

    A.   Jazz

    B.   The Blues

    C.   Dancing

VII. Baby or Child Love

    A.   Violet's desire for a baby and what it does to her

    B.   True Belle's love for her grandchildren

Conclusion: *Jazz* is a realistic love story because it goes beyond the traditional love between a man and a woman to discuss many other types of love.

Topic #2

The work of writers like F. Scott Fitzgerald, Sinclair Lewis, and Ernest Hemingway looked at American lifestyles and attitudes in the Jazz Age. How does Toni Morrison's *Jazz* add another dimension to the existing work on American life in this decade?

Outline

I.   Thesis Statement: *By writing about rural African-Americans, The Great Migration, and the racism African-Americans experi-*

enced in the North, Morrison paints a broader picture of life in the 1920s.

II.   The Traditional Image of the 1920s

   A.   Prosperity

   B.   Attitudes

III. The African-American Experience in the 1920s

   A.   Difficulties of Southern life

      1.   Segregation

      2.   Sharecropping

      3.   Ku Klux Klan

   B.   The Great Migration

      1.   Dignity

      2.   Opportunity

   C.   The climate of fear

      1.   Lynchings

      2.   Race riots

      3.   Discrimination

Conclusion: Morrison's portrayal of African-American life in the 1920s completes the picture of American life during this decade.

Topic #3

Music is used as a backdrop for the novel. Instead of being titled *Jazz*, why could this novel have been named "The Blues"?

Outline

I.   Thesis Statement: *This novel could have easily been named "The Blues" because many characters have sad, sad stories to tell.*

II. The Blues Defined

   A.   Origins

      B.   Examples

III.   Violet's Blues

      A.   Joe's affair

      B.   Her mother's suicide

      C.   Her father's disappearance

      D.   Baby hunger

IV.   Joe's Blues

      A.   Violet

      B.   Dorcas

      C.   His mother

V.   Dorcas' Blues

      A.   Her parents

      B.   Aunt Alice

      C.   Joe

VI.   Rose Dear's Blues

      A.   Caring for her children

      B.   Her husband

VII.   Golden Gray's Blues

      A.   His parentage

      B.   The changes that would take place in his life

VIII. The Narrator's Blues

      A.   No life

      B.   Never experienced a love like Violet and Joe's

Conclusion: Almost every character in *Jazz* could be said to have the blues.

Topic #4

The North as the "promised land" is a reocurring theme in African-American history and literature. Compare and contrast what the promised land meant during slavery and post-slavery.

Outline

I.   Thesis Statement: *The North was considered the promised land because it was the one place where African-Americans hoped they could find freedom and opportunity.*

II. The Promised Land

    A.   Origins as a biblical term

    B.   Heaven on earth

III. The Promised Land During Slavery

    A.   Escape to freedom

    B.   The Underground Railroad

    C.   Harriet Tubman

IV. The Promised Land During Post-slavery

    A.   The Great Migration

        1.   Escape from slavery

        2.   Economic opportunity

        3.   Dignity

    B.   Northern realities

        1.   Racism in other forms

        2.   Poor housing

        3.   The impact of city life

Conclusion: For African-Americans, the North was viewed as the promised land because it offered freedom from slavery at one point and freedom from political and economic hardships at another.

Topic #5

Alice Manfred reacts very strongly to the march protesting the killings in East St. Louis, Illinois. Discuss her reaction and the kinds of reactions that could be expected from various segments of the

American population.

Outline

I.   Thesis Statement: *There were many different reactions to the killings and the protest march that followed.*

II. Reactions by Residents of East St. Louis

    A.   African-American

    B.   White

III. Reactions by New Yorkers

    A.   Harlemites

    B.   Whites

IV. Public Opinion Throughout the United States

    A.   North

    B.   South

    C.   African-American

    D.   White

V.   Personal Reactions

    A.   Alice Manfred

    B.   Dorcas

    C.   Joe

Conclusion: The reaction to the riots and killings in East St. Louis, Illinois depended largely on race and political views.

SECTION FOUR

Bibliography

Adams, Russell L. *Great Negroes Past and Present*. Chicago: Afro-Am, 1984.

Adero, Malaika. ed. *Up South*. New York: The New Press, 1993.

Angelo, Bonnie. "The Pain of Being Black." *Time* (May 22, 1989): 120-122.

Bloom Harold. *Modern Critical Views: Toni Morrison*. New York: Chelsea House, 1990.

Boardman, Fon W. *America and the Jazz Age*. New York: Henry Z. Walck, 1968.

Dreifus, Claudia. "Chole Wofford Talks About Toni Morrison," *New York Times Magazine* (September 11, 1994).

Eden, Richard. "Those Nights on the Harlem Roof Tops," *Los Angeles Times Book Review* (April 19, 1992): 3.

Katz, William Loren. *Eyewitness: The Negro in American History*. New York: Pitman Publishing, 1969.

Leonard, John. "All That Jazz." *New York* (December 21-28, 1992): 72.

Mendelsholm, Jane. "Harlem on Her Mind," *Voice Literary Supplement*, (May 1992): 25

Nicholson, David. "Toni Morrison's Rhapsody in Blues", *The Washington Post Book World* (April 19, 1992).

O'Brien, Edna. "The Clearest Eye: Jazz," *New York Times Review of Books* (April 5, 1992).

Potter, L., Miles, W. Rosenblum, N. *Liberators: Fighting on Two Fronts in WWII.* New York: Harcourt Brace Jovanovich, 1992.

"The World According to Toni Morrison," *Essence* (May 1995).

"Toni Morrison's Black Magic," *Newsweek* (March 30, 1981): 51.

Wilson, Joan Hoff. *The Twenties.* Boston: Little, Brown & Co., 1972.

MAXnotes®

REA's Literature Study Guides

MAXnotes® are student-friendly. They offer a fresh look at masterpieces of literature, presented in a lively and interesting fashion. **MAXnotes®** offer the essentials of what you should know about the work, including outlines, explanations and discussions of the plot, character lists, analyses, and historical context. **MAXnotes®** are designed to help you think independently about literary works by raising various issues and thought-provoking ideas and questions. Written by literary experts who currently teach the subject, **MAXnotes®** enhance your understanding and enjoyment of the work.

Available **MAXnotes®** include the following:

Absalom, Absalom!	Heart of Darkness	Of Mice and Men
The Aeneid of Virgil	Henry IV, Part I	On the Road
Animal Farm	Henry V	Othello
Antony and Cleopatra	The House on Mango Street	Paradise Lost
As I Lay Dying	Huckleberry Finn	A Passage to India
As You Like It	I Know Why the Caged	Plato's Republic
The Autobiography of	Bird Sings	Portrait of a Lady
Malcolm X	The Iliad	A Portrait of the Artist
The Awakening	Invisible Man	as a Young Man
Beloved	Jane Eyre	Pride and Prejudice
Beowulf	Jazz	A Raisin in the Sun
Billy Budd	The Joy Luck Club	Richard II
The Bluest Eye, A Novel	Jude the Obscure	Romeo and Juliet
Brave New World	Julius Caesar	The Scarlet Letter
The Canterbury Tales	King Lear	Sir Gawain and the
The Catcher in the Rye	Les Misérables	Green Knight
The Color Purple	Lord of the Flies	Slaughterhouse-Five
The Crucible	Macbeth	Song of Solomon
Death in Venice	The Merchant of Venice	The Sound and the Fury
Death of a Salesman	The Metamorphoses of Ovid	The Stranger
The Divine Comedy I: Inferno	The Metamorphosis	The Sun Also Rises
Dubliners	Middlemarch	A Tale of Two Cities
Emma	A Midsummer Night's Dream	Taming of the Shrew
Euripedes' Electra & Medea	Moby-Dick	The Tempest
Frankenstein	Moll Flanders	Tess of the D'Urbervilles
Gone with the Wind	Mrs. Dalloway	Their Eyes Were Watching God
The Grapes of Wrath	Much Ado About Nothing	To Kill a Mockingbird
Great Expectations	My Antonia	To the Lighthouse
The Great Gatsby	Native Son	Twelfth Night
Gulliver's Travels	1984	Uncle Tom's Cabin
Hamlet	The Odyssey	Waiting for Godot
Hard Times	Oedipus Trilogy	Wuthering Heights

RESEARCH & EDUCATION ASSOCIATION
61 Ethel Road W. • Piscataway, New Jersey 08854
Phone: (908) 819-8880

Please send me more information about MAXnotes®.

Name _____

Address _____

City _____ State _____ Zip _____